CRAZY LOVE
AN AUTOBIOGRAPHICAL ACCOUNT OF MARRIAGE AND MADNESS

CRAZY LOVE

AN AUTOBIOGRAPHICAL ACCOUNT OF MARRIAGE AND MADNESS

PHYLLIS NAYLOR

WILLIAM MORROW AND COMPANY, INC.

NEW YORK 1977

Printed in the United States of America.

1   2   3   4   5   6   7   8   9   10

Library of Congress Cataloging in Publication Data

Naylor, Phyllis Reynolds.
    Crazy love.

        1. Naylor, Phyllis Reynolds. 2. Mental
illness—Biography. I. Title.
RC464.N37A34   616.8'97'09 [B]   76-56359
ISBN 0-688-03178-1

BOOK DESIGN   CARL WEISS

To

J. ALFRED PRUFROCK

AND

ALL WHO HELPED

This is a true story. Because of my desire not to embarrass the people involved, I have changed some of the names and places. But the events and dialogue are reported faithfully.

ONE

THERE IS A BIRTHMARK in the center of my right buttock, a dark brown spot the size of a dime, surrounded by a larger ring of light brown, surrounded by a great expanse of white flesh. This whole piece of my anatomy resembles a huge eye—dark pupil, white eyeball—staring out at the world from behind me, veiled by underthings. When I was small, a neighbor once jovially referred to the mark as my rotten spot. I asked my mother if a man would ever marry me in spite of it, and she answered that my husband would love me so much that the birthmark wouldn't matter. She was wrong. It drove him mad.

Or was it something else—some warp in the chromosomes, some flaw in the genes, a thin film of paranoia in the embryonic sac? Was it the University or Mozart's *Requiem* or the full moon or the Mafia? Was it our wedding night, perhaps—that destroyer of great expectations? Or does madness always begin on a day that is otherwise normal—beautiful, even—fate thumbing its nose at the future?

The lake was rimmed, on its southern edge, by flat gray boulders. We had spent the morning ambling hand in hand over the rocks, dodging the puddles in the shallow pockets where the water sloshed up through the crevices. Ted had been admitted to the graduate school at the University, majoring in something called Quantitative Inquiry, and life was going reasonably well. Then he said it:

"Dr. Gerber knows about your birthmark."

I remember how silly and innocent it seemed—no more important than a small lump on the side of the neck or a breeze that comes up out of nowhere—a yellow haze, perhaps, on a day that is strangely still. I laughed, and later—remembering that laughter—thought of the great mechanical face on top of a fun house, nodding and shrieking its "Ha, ha, ha," to a deserted sidewalk.

How could Ted's adviser possibly know about my birthmark? And why on earth would he care?

"What did Dr. Gerber say?" I prodded, but Ted was evasive. He wasn't sure—a reference, perhaps; an innuendo. I laughed again, Ted smiled, and we let the matter drop.

The following afternoon we were driving home from a shopping trip when Ted said suddenly, "Dr. Gerber has been following us for six blocks."

"Maybe he lives around here," I offered disinterestedly.

"No," Ted said, "that's not it." He swung the car over to the curb and stopped, allowing the Plymouth behind us to pass. I glanced at the driver, expecting to see the sharp, angular profile of Dr. Gerber. The man in the Plymouth was black and somewhat overweight.

"You must be studying too hard," I joked. It didn't particularly bother me that Ted did not respond.

As I put the groceries away, I remembered an incident

10

that had taken place a few months earlier. Ted had received an assistantship that involved working out research computations on a calculator. He was expected to spend a certain number of hours a week in an office at the University. One particular Saturday, I had suggested that I go with him and bring a picnic lunch. Because I free-lanced in my spare time, I could easily spend the two hours writing in one corner of the room while he worked. Then we would have lunch out on the campus.

About eleven o'clock we'd looked up suddenly to see Dr. Gerber standing in the doorway staring fiercely at me. I don't remember whether Ted spoke or whether we both sat mute. Dr. Gerber stalked away, and Ted was upset because he had evidently used poor judgment in allowing me to come. I never came again.

We could have been copulating on the table, however. We could have been drinking beer over the data and dropping crumbs on the calculator, but this seemingly made no difference. Though Dr. Gerber did not mention it again, Ted remembered. Perhaps it was here that the seed was sown. Dr. Gerber resented me; Ted was sure of it.

I did not see a pattern in the strangeness until the third day. When dinner was over, Ted seemed unusually restless and preoccupied. He stood at the front window of our efficiency apartment, looking nervously out over the boulevard, and then checked the fire escape at the back. I remembered thinking, as I took my bath, that two more years of tenseness for a Ph.D. wasn't worth it. Two more years of worrying about what Dr. Gerber thought, Dr. Jacobs thought, Dr. Blum thought, two more years of the obsessive work habits—checking and rechecking, copying and recopying, reading and rereading—that seemed to be so characteristic of Ted.

When I came out of the bathroom, I noticed that Ted

11

had already converted the sofa into our bed and was down on his hands and knees behind it.

"What are you looking for?"

He did not answer right away, but seemed annoyed. "Something's going on around here, and I'm going to find out what." He lifted the mattress and scanned the springs, then frisked the pillows with both hands.

I decided that something had happened at the University which was very upsetting to Ted—a huge misunderstanding, a weird coincidence that could be fully explained if he would just tell me about it.

I sat down on the bed. "What's wrong with you lately? You haven't been yourself and you know it."

He smiled cynically. "*You* tell *me*."

"What do you mean? What are you talking about?"

The words came grudgingly. It had something to do with role playing, Ted said. Every day one of his professors, first Gerber, then Blum, would imitate Ted's parents, either by gesture or inflection or in some other way which was detectable only by Ted. They were testing him, he said, to see if he were really Ph.D. material—to see if he could take it.

I stared at him, unbelieving. The professors did not even know his parents. Was it possible that they could resent this Italian student in their classes, and be trying to drive him out by subtle ridicule? Did you have to be 100 percent Jewish to belong to the graduate elite? Had we really displeased Dr. Gerber that much? Had he talked with the other professors and decided that Ted should be made as uncomfortable as possible so he would leave of his own accord? What sacred rule had we violated that would make them hate us so?

Whatever the professors were doing or saying, however, Ted was exaggerating it out of all proportion, I was sure. I tried to make a joke of it. Why should they go to all that

12

trouble? Why not just lock Ted up in a room under Gerber's fierce stare and see if he would crack? That would be infinitely faster.

Ted was not amused. As I watched him feverishly searching around the rug, pouncing on any ripple or bulge, I felt the first real flicker of fear, a fear that would move in with me and be a constant companion during the next three years.

"What does all this have to do with our apartment, our bed?" I asked numbly.

Because, Ted explained, every day one of the professors let drop a little hint as to what Ted and I had talked about the night before—a veiled reference to our conversations, our plans.

I was sure that if I heard it I would interpret it differently. "Give me an example," I urged. "Tell me exactly what was said."

But Ted couldn't. It was vague, he said, far too subtle. Only he could understand it.

I laughed angrily, furious at the silliness. It was all too ridiculous, I told him. He talked as though he were cracking up. Ted smiled too, a little sheepishly, and changed the subject.

And so we went to bed, talked some more of this and that, and Ted drew me to him. If his hands seemed to wander somewhat distractedly over my body, I didn't notice; if his movements seemed more rigid, more controlled, I was not aware of it. But suddenly, at the height of our lovemaking, I was startled by Ted's hand over my mouth and his tense voice whispered, "Shhhhh. Not so loud. They'll hear you."

Why did I think that, with time, things would get better, that given a week or a month the misunderstanding, the anxiety, would disappear? Whoever conferred a medical de-

13

gree on the mere passage of minutes and hours? What wild sense of optimism made me believe that merely because a man is brilliant he is assured of success, or that a loyal wife could pull him through whatever purgatory he had chosen for himself? Where did I get my unshakable faith in institutions, and my calm conviction that Gerber, Jacobs, and Blum would protect their graduate students unto the death, even from themselves? And what would I have thought if, lying next to Ted and wondering who all his "they" included, I could have known that the next three years would be infinitely more frightening?

We met when I was seventeen and Ted was twenty-five, and married a year later. What attracted him was a mystery, for he glimpsed me first in wrinkled pants and an old tee shirt. Raw material, that's what he saw. Eliza Doolittle.

Our home town itself was as incongruous as we were. Originally named Ophelia (a neighboring burg was called Hamlet), this delicately conceived city was actually an industrial center renowned for its police force. Somehow, over the years, someone had the good sense to rename it Oakton. Ted had been born there; I was an immigrant from Indiana, and our houses were only a block apart.

Could a White-Anglo-Saxon-Protestant girl find love with the son of an Italian life-insurance salesman and a converted Jewess? Ted was slim, tall, and—despite his compulsiveness —studiously handsome to a girl who longed for a college man of her very own. His hair was very dark, with a deep wave on one side, and his nose very straight. He knew the train connections between Oakton and the University, and how to get around once I reached the campus. He showed me the University library, the chapel, the hospital, and described the architecture of each. He could talk for twenty hours on any subject known to Western man, and fifty

14

hours on literature, music, or philosophy in particular. He was reading encyclopedias before I was even conceived. He knew the major works of Brahms while I was still being rocked to sleep to the "Lullaby." He had read the complete works of Shakespeare, underlined passages throughout, dissected each play into meticulously typed notes on plot, characterization, theme, inferences, the meanings of the ambiguities, the ambiguities of the meanings, the similarities, the differences, the metaphors, the philosophical ideas, until he had so thoroughly digested the playwright there was little left to discover—or so it seemed to me.

A straight-A student in grade and high school, he had served at the end of World War II as a navigator in the Air Force. Now he was entering his fourth year at the University, majoring in English literature, and I had dropped into his life like a seed on fertile soil.

And what had I to offer this superlative of academia? Of English-German background, I was average in height and weight, brown-haired, green-eyed, pretty, but no beauty. To Ted's IQ of 184, I brought a B average. To his intimate knowledge of baroque music, I brought a decade of Monday nights spent listening to the *Firestone Program* and the *Bell Telephone Hour* with my family, the zenith, we thought, of great music (that and Saturday afternoon opera). To Ted's gleaming leather-bound *Harvard Classics,* I contributed some worn volumes of Mark Twain which my father had read to us. I had never heard of Schopenhauer, Dostoevski, or Khachaturian. I knew almost nothing of Sigmund Freud. The farthest I had ever traveled from our home in the Midwest was Louisiana. I could not drive, type, cook, or dance, and had never signed a check in my life. A real bargain.

It was worse than that. I was the antithesis of Ted's most personal traits. Where he was compulsive, I was obsessively

15

careless; where he was precise, I wandered all over the map. The only thing I had ever done with reasonable success was write, which I enjoyed in private. I had published a few stories and made a brief debut in my senior year as class poet at the graduation exercises, and then went underground again.

I hungrily read the books Ted loaned me, but never in the way he wanted. I never underlined or copied passages. I never made lists of characters or relationships or biographical facts. I would fling myself headlong into the chapters, even reading the last one first if I felt so inclined. As our attraction deepened, Ted gave me a collection of Mozart piano sonatas, and I tackled anything that had less than three sharps and three flats. I made up the rhythm as I went along, and if I came to a difficult passage, I simply left it out. Perhaps it was that which drove him mad.

Mine was the most ordinary family in the entire Midwest. Whenever people wrote about middle-class values, mores, income, or politics, that was my family they were talking about. A walking Norman Rockwell portfolio, that was us. We were descended on both sides from a long line of teachers, preachers, and farmers. My father worked as a salesman for various companies, beginning with H. J. Heinz in the Depression, symbolized by a giant pickle. All through our childhood he was so loyal that I didn't discover Campbell's soups until I was married. As he changed jobs, we changed houses, and by the time I entered high school, we had lived in eight different neighborhoods, stretching across Indiana, Illinois, and Iowa. And that's where our personalities developed. Like the roads in Iowa as seen from a plane, all coming together at perfect right angles, the men and women of American Gothic lived their lives square and true.

We were raised not to think but to be sensitive to what we suspected everybody else was thinking. We were the original other-directed family, with supple spines ready to bend at a moment's notice. What will the doctor think if you cry (that it hurts, maybe?)? What will the teacher think if your knees are dirty? What will Grandma think if she doesn't hear from us soon? What will the minister think if we're late again? What will the neighbors think if they see you and Ted kissing on the porch?

We became master detectives of everyone's feelings but our own. We watched facial expressions for the slightest hint of disapproval. We knew what someone needed before he even asked. We were Pavlov's dogs, ready to snap to attention at the sound of the bell.

As members of my mother's JOY club, which she organized for pre-teens, we bravely recited our slogan: "Jesus first, Others next, Yourself last." We were always last. I grew up supremely confident of my own unimportance.

It was not just the five of us—mother, father, three children—who were ordinary, however. Counting all blood relatives on both sides—forty-four aunts, uncles, cousins, and grandparents—no one had ever been in jail. No one had ever been arrested, molested, or raped. No one had ever had heart disease, diabetes, or tuberculosis. No one got his picture in *Look* or *Life*. When two of my uncles founded a manufacturing company for heavy equipment, we finally had a success story to recount again and again over the ham and biscuits at family reunions. And when one of my aunts married a man who later robbed this company (he was apprehended making his getaway at seven miles an hour in the huge orange crane he had stolen), we had a scandal, too, of our very own.

Bragging, however, was permissible only if success were attributed to (1) God; (2) a marvelous teacher; (3) luck. Talent was attributable only to (1) a marvelous teacher; (2) a relative whom you resembled; (3) a gift. The notion that

17

anyone may have succeeded because he worked ten times harder than anybody else was frowned upon—there had to be an outside influence, preferably supernatural. Conceit was the ultimate sin, and therefore compliments were kept to a minimum.

The children thus raised in humility were consequently ravenous for praise and jealous of each other. We quarreled both openly and deviously for our parents' attention. Who does Daddy love most? Older sister? Younger sister? Little brother? None of the above. Daddy loves himself best.

My father was the undisputed ruler of our home in things that mattered to him. If they did not matter, he left them to my mother. Perhaps the fact that the household revolved around him was not the result so much of male chauvinism as it was of the Depression. It was he, after all, whose salary determined where we lived and what we ate, and the income, in turn, depended entirely on whether he made a sale. Meals were scheduled at his convenience and were planned around his ulcer. An hour of quiet time was reserved each evening so that he could fill out his reports. His underwear and shirts were meticulously laundered, and when I was old enough to iron the handkerchief he wore in his breast pocket, I was told how important it was that the edges come together perfectly. Every potential customer, I was sure, accepted or declined on the basis of my father's pocket handkerchief, and ironing the edges gave me a feeling that I was doing my bit.

My whole unverbalized hope in growing up was to match my sister's accomplishments and become as beloved as my brother. My sister made the honor roll, the madrigals, the operetta, and the senior play. I made the honor roll, the madrigals, the operetta, and the senior play. My sister took three years of art and painted in oils. I took three years of art and painted in oils. My sister talked the school into letting her drop home economics to take Latin instead. I went to the superintendent and asked to drop home economics and take Latin instead. (I have never yet met a person who greeted me with *Gallia est omnis divisa in partes tres,* but I have met several who wished I could cook.)

I was never as pretty in my sister's hand-me-downs as she had been, and felt that I was destined forever to trying harder because I was Number 2. It never occurred to me that I had a choice, or that there were other things worth doing she might never have tried. This, then, was the state of my psyche when I met Ted. He was not only older than the man my sister had married, but he knew more than my forty-four relatives put together. He talked of Socrates and Plato; he hummed concertos and fugues; he recited passages from Balzac and Thackeray; and—most of all—he wanted me. I gave in without a whimper.

If it seemed unlikely that Ted and I should have fallen in love, it was even more amazing that his parents had.

Mr. Moreno had left a beautiful red-haired wife and daughter in Italy to come to the states and seek his fortune. He found it, more or less, in the life insurance business. His wife, however, refused to follow him, and that was all he would ever tell anyone about the matter.

He was a short, slight man, who dressed in conservative suits and vests, topped with a wide-brimmed hat, and bore a vague resemblance to Harry Truman. His face was permanently etched in a frozen smile. By slight twists and turns of the corners of his mouth, however, it became a smile of pleasure, a smile of suspicion, a smile of sarcasm, a smile of wrath, depending on his mood. Some people look as though they are laughing even when they cry, and vice versa. That was Mr. Moreno.

Ted's father was a man who liked things orderly and accounted for. There was only one right way to do anything

19

and an allotted amount of time for each. He taught Ted to brush his teeth to a mental count of eighteen, comb his hair to a count of seven. He allowed only so many minutes for washing and dressing, and had a set time for moving the bowels. Ted recounted these compulsions to me in both derision and anger, yet they continued to influence him in spite of himself.

In a quiet neighborhood where most cars remained on the street overnight, Mr. Moreno not only parked his in the garage but padlocked the door as well. It was no accident that he had built their house far back from the road, hidden behind another, with a "Private: No Trespassing" sign at the driveway. As for his relationship with Ted's mother, his second wife, all he would say of her was that she was a "good woman."

The Good Woman herself was several years older than her husband and heavier. Whereas Mr. Moreno walked ramrod straight, his wife walked with her head hanging forward, as though the weight of her enormous brain was too much to hold up. Her eyes were very small and quick, and her nose, like Ted's, very straight. She had heavy legs and thick ankles and walked ponderously, with her toes pointing outward. While Ted's father talked rapidly in Italian accents, Mrs. Moreno spoke didactically in deep resounding tones. She had such an air of authority that one could not come away from her unimpressed. It was like being in the presence of Golda Meir.

She had met Ted's father in a veteran's hospital where he was suffering the effects of having been gassed and left for dead in the First World War. According to Mrs. Moreno, the doctors gave him only six months to live, so she married him. Surprise. Thirty years later he was still going strong.

Mrs. Moreno had been married twice before and survived both husbands. By the first, she had a daughter who developed schizophrenia and died in a mental hospital at age thirty. By the second she had a son who ran away at sixteen and kept his sanity. By the third, she had Ted. And somewhere along the way she became a convert for Christ.

Recent converts make marvelously enthusiastic evangelists. Mrs. Moreno fervently believed that her mission in life was to proselytize among her friends, which must have made her wildly popular at the delicatessen. She carried a number of tracts in her purse which she passed out on almost any occasion at all. She had dozens of instant sermons, ready at a moment's notice. And she had a limitless supply of prayers which were offered on her knees, aloud, for the rest of the family to enjoy. The two which Ted remembered most vividly from childhood were prayers that God would punish her enemies and that the Almighty, who could move mountains, would move her bowels as well.

Aside from turning Jews into Gentiles, Mrs. Moreno's time and energy were spent worrying about her digestive system. Nutrition was the science of determining which foods were laxative and which were constipating. ("Spinach," Ted used to mimic, "is the broom of the intestines.") Elimination was almost as sacred a ritual as Holy Communion. When she felt the spirit move her, Mrs. M. would retire to the bathroom, closing both kitchen and hallway doors behind her, and after a considerable length of time, she emerged either victorious or in need of more prayer. As evidence of her holiness, moreover, she once remarked to Ted that her excrement, miraculously, had no odor.

Into this household, then, Ted was born—a child to compensate for Mr. Moreno's daughter left in Italy and Mrs. Moreno's own two children. Not only was he small and helpless and theirs, but intelligent beyond their dreams. At three, according to his mother, he was reading the encyclopedia. At four he was amazing the neighbors with his extraordinary vocabulary. At five, he was astounding his teachers (like Christ in the temple at twelve!) with his wisdom.

According to Ted, there was a Yiddish greeting used between pregnant Orthodox women, *"Zo iahzun zein dê Meshiach,"* which translated into, "May your son be the Messiah." Exactly what Mrs. Moreno believed in this regard is unclear. Over her bed, however, she had a picture which she insisted was the only known portrait of Christ—a strange-looking profile which, upon closer inspection, looked suspiciously like her own. She also had a recurring dream:

"In a conference room in the greatest city of the world, the most famous scientists are gathered to present an award to the one who has done the most for mankind. But as Ted stands up to receive it, a door opens near the back, and an elderly couple, bent with age, make their way slowly to the front. Turning to the distinguished scientists, who have risen out of respect, Ted says softly, 'Gentlemen, my parents.' "

There was more I didn't learn until later. Mrs. Moreno had some very strange ideas about mothering. When Ted was still a baby, she confided to me, she would wait until he cried for his bottle and then set it just out of reach. Why? To teach him patience. As for friends and parties and fun, he had no time for it, she insisted. He was much too busy studying. And when he reached high school, she absolutely forbade him to date.

"Why?" I asked.

"Because so many of the girls were getting pregnant."

An epidemic, maybe? I asked Ted later. Two, he told me.

Ted himself ran away once. He fled to the home of his Latin teacher who told him that her apartment could be only a temporary refuge. And so he returned.

Mrs. Moreno, however, insisted that Ted had eyes only for her, and she kept an eagle eye of her own on all the young ladies her son overlooked, with an audible remark about each of them: "Her arms are too fat." "Her chin's too big." "Her legs are skinny."

He remarked once that had his parents beat or physically abused him, the authorities could have stepped in and taken him away. But because the abuse was emotional, and the damage was done to the mind, there were no laws to protect him at all.

But then things changed. The Second World War came and Ted enlisted. He was stationed in England and met a girl there. He slept in barracks with the other men, marched to their music and sang their songs ("Roll over, Mabel; you're better on the oth-er side. Ta da!"). When the war was over, he entered the University. He was placed in Ramley House, a dormitory for veterans going to school on the GI bill. The umbilical cord had been stretched to the breaking point.

And then we met. I had been sent to his home on an errand for my mother. Expecting to find two elderly people, I was embarrassed to discover a quiet young man smiling at me against the background of a Brandenburg Concerto, and the following day he came to my house and invited me out.

His mother, he told me later, had been telling him about my beautiful older sister, who was, of course, safely married. But his father had said, "If I were you, Ted, I'd keep my eye on the younger one."

I wanted to like them both. I looked at Ted's parents as one looks at her lover, excusing faults, explaining peculiarities, ignoring what could neither be excused nor explained. That Ted himself had no wish to be like either of them seemed assurance enough. Our love was like a cocoon that would protect us from everything.

Old love letters are frequently painful, especially if all the things promised seldom came true. Especially if the girl who wrote, "Our nights together will be so wonderful," turned out to be miserable, and the man who said, "When you're safe in my arms, nothing will ever be able to hurt you," became a patient on a locked ward.

Our courtship, chaste and idealistic, began just before Ted returned to the University for the fall quarter and I began my senior year in high school. Excerpts from our first stuffy letters proved that we deserved each other:

HE: I observed the people on campus for several hours yester-day. Most are deceiving themselves, but their posturing is transparent. They have not learned to separate honest questioning from cynicism. Too many are scholars, not students, pedants, not men. I cannot accept such an ivory tower view of life.

SHE: I'm determined that nothing will affect our happiness. I will never argue with you. If I find that our talk is leading to an argument, I will stop talking.

The formality, however, soon gave way to romanticism. We worshiped each other and our idealized picture of what life had in store for us:

HE: As many times as I've stroked your hair, my darling, I never remembered seeing red in it. I'm thrilled with the discovery. You delight me with your little turned-up nose and your soft voice, your slim arms and your joy in children. . . .

SHE: You know, darling, some of the happiest times in our marriage will be the mornings our six children run into our bedroom to wake us up and they all snuggle down under the covers and we'll talk awhile before breakfast.

24

HE: Our souls sang love songs when we walked together Saturday morning and yesterday outside the chapel—the whole
weekend, in fact. . . . It's snowing now, and you should be
here where you belong. When we're husband and wife, you
won't mind the cold, or even feel it. Has anyone ever loved
as much as we?

My rapture over Ted's letters was only slightly diminished
when he confessed later that he always made a rough draft
first and copied them over. As the months passed, we began
to feel more at ease with each other. Ted was possessive of
me, and I loved it. He wanted to know every detail of my
life. No one had ever seemed to care that much before:

HE: Being stodgy and acting like an old married couple isn't
much fun. I'm warning you, darling, when we're husband
and wife we won't ever act like old married folks. I'm going
to bed contented tonight, as contented, that is, as old bache-
lors can ever be. Some day bedtimes will be a delight for us
both.

SHE: Today in history I got my first well-deserved scolding
for day-dreaming in class. I wanted so very much to tell Mr.
Evans that I was in love and had someone wonderful to
think about, but I doubt if that would have helped.

HE: I have no objection to your physical fitness class in gym,
but they'd better not make a muscle-woman out of my girl.
I simply won't have them tinkering with your measurements.
I've never noticed that your arms and waist are too skinny,
or that you need to lose weight anywhere else. I have the
final say, and you can tell them that. Your measurements
please me the way they are.

As many weekends as he could manage, Ted came home
and we spent what time we could together. But his im-
patience with the University became more and more evident:

OCTOBER 9:   I just went to the Bursar's office to fill out some
more papers regarding my tuition. (Bursars are gnome-like
creatures who collect and hoard the students' money.)

OCTOBER 11: The readings I have been assigned this quarter are lifeless in comparison with your letters. So much of the warmth in my life these days comes from Oakton. I'm terribly disenchanted with the University.

OCTOBER 23: There are six of us including the professor in English 318A, Studies in Modern English Literature. The word "modern" must be taken in the usual University sense —you have ancient, medieval, and then modern. To be more precise, it is a course in the phonology, morphology, and syntax of the English language between the years 1650 and 1800.

NOVEMBER 6: I am working on another paper for Dr. Sloan's course, and must finish it tonight. The topic is the uses and meanings of the word *Gothic,* from 1650 to 1800. So far, it seems to be going well.

NOVEMBER 8: I have been having a discussion with some other English lit majors about the department here. It is generally agreed that the method used to teach literature is too rational and too intensive. It simply is not wide or appreciative enough.

NOVEMBER 20: Positively scintillating, the wit at this school. I just overheard the following exchange in the washroom:
Student A: I wouldn't be shaving these whiskers off if I knew Senator McCarthy wouldn't be around.
Student B: What's the matter? Your hair isn't red, is it?

DECEMBER 4: The University has been unhealthy for me this quarter. When I think of the shape that the world is in, I feel that everything is out of joint, but I can't blame society for my own problems.

DECEMBER 11: Phyllis, I'm quite certain I don't want a Ph.D. in English. Perhaps I will eventually decide to get one in education, though. At least that would turn me in the direction I need to go, closer to humanity and away from books. Do you know, I've never lived for the future as much as I have lately? Since I met you, sweetheart, my musical tastes have shifted from Beethoven to Haydn. Beethoven is now too serious for me at times. I prefer Haydn, who is more joyful, and certainly shows greater balance. Dearest Phyl, warm Phyl, my Phyl, I dream of the delight of possessing you. Only four more days and you will be in my arms again. I will hold you so tightly you will have to plead to get out.

TWO

THE THING ABOUT "THEY" is that the list grew daily. First it was only Dr. Gerber, and then it became the whole department. The custodian in the basement of our building was suspect, as well as the druggist on the corner. Everyone, it seemed, was in on the testing process, to see if this man, or any man so conceived and so dedicated, could long endure. Nothing short of ordeal by water and fire would convince them that Ted was truly Ph.D. material.

Even the mailman and the car mechanic spoke in double-entendre. A statement as simple as, "Not so cloudy today, is it?" was full of significance: a sign, perhaps, that the worst was over; a trick to catch Ted off guard; a suggestion, a threat, a warning. . . . Some remarks, he believed, were made deliberately confusing, and so he would withdraw for long periods, musing over what they might mean. Every gesture, every grimace, was designed to test his reactions.

Consequently, the slightest action on his part had a million ramifications: should he sit on the right or left side of the room? wear brown shoes or black? use a pencil or write with ink? drive down Kimball Road or Bradley? The possibilities were unlimited. He was obsessed with T.S. Eliot, reciting lines aloud to no one in particular, and became one with J. Alfred Prufrock:

> And indeed there will be time
> To wonder, "Do I dare?" and, "Do I dare?"
> Time to turn back and descend the stair,
> With a bald spot in the middle of my hair—

What had happened to the college man in the soft sweaters who carried books beneath one arm? What had happened to the man who had promised to protect me always, who said he would make me burst with happiness, who wrote that I was like candlelight and homemade bread, and said that our love would be the most beautiful experience of our lives?

Ted was no raving maniac. He went to the University each morning and grocery shopping with me on Saturdays, carried on small talk with friends and neighbors when we met on the street. Others saw him as somewhat nervous—a little distracted, maybe—but certainly friendly. To me, however, there was a decided change—a strange cracking of the knuckles, a pointless pacing, the furtive look in his eyes, and the sardonic, knowing nature of his smile.

It was five years from the day we married to the time the symptoms first began. A live-in psychiatrist would undoubtedly have seen symptoms long before they became evident to me—the isolated child who preferred books to playmates; the solitary youth whose social life consisted of his Latin teacher; the loner listening to a Haydn quartet against a background of quarreling parents who battled for dominance.

Having come from a home where parents avoided disagreements to the point of pathology, I was unprepared for the atmosphere in Ted's home when I visited there before our marriage. I felt as though we were all perched on a great high wire, and that the slightest murmur, the smallest sneeze, could send us all spinning.

It was a neat house, compulsively clean, everything in perfect order. I would be greeted with a great show of cordiality and what passed for joshing between the older Morenos. And then, to an accompaniment of Bach, the conversation would begin. They insisted on answering for me:

MR. MORENO: How far you been, Phyllis? Ever go to Italy?

THE GOOD WOMAN: She's only seventeen, Ted. When would she have had time to travel? She's still a student.

MR. MORENO: So don't some students travel? You think nobody go to Italy?

THE GOOD WOMAN: Of course people go to Italy. But it's not the only country in the world.

MR. MORENO: You think I don't know that? You think I don't know about the world? You think I fight in the war and don't know about the world?

THE GOOD WOMAN: Travel isn't necessarily an education, you know. A person can go right through a country and not know as much about it as someone who studies it thoroughly in a book.

MR. MORENO (beginning to shout): You think books tell all about Italy, you don't know Italy! You think books tell how it is to be gassed and left for dead out in the field? You think books tell all about war? You think . . .

TED: Would you mind debating somewhere else so Phyllis and I can hear this partita?

THE GOOD WOMAN: Phyllis, dear, let me make you a sandwich or something.

MR. MORENO: She don't wanna eat anything. She just had dinner, maybe. It's hot day, she like something to drink.

THE GOOD WOMAN: I didn't ask you, I asked Phyllis.

MR. MORENO: And I'm telling you it's hot—better for something with ice. Besides, Phyllis don't eat lots. You can tell she don't eat on hot day.

THE GOOD WOMAN: It's easy to be slim before you've had children. You won't believe it, Phyllis, but I had an eighteen-inch waist when I was your age.

MR. MORENO (chuckling): No, Phyllis don't believe that. I don't believe that. Nobody's going to believe that.

THE GOOD WOMAN: That's because you didn't know me then. I had the smallest waist of all the girls I knew. I was a real beauty then. It's a pity you didn't know me. . . .

MR. MORENO: Did I say you weren't a beauty? I said I don't believe you had eighteen-inch waist. Twenty, maybe.

THE GOOD WOMAN: So what did you know about me? What did . . . ?

TED: Look, I don't care about your waist. I don't care about Italy. Would you just be quiet so we can hear this music?

THE GOOD WOMAN: You see how he talks to us, Phyllis?

MR. MORENO: Maybe she'll teach him some manners.

This was not a quarrel, Ted explained later. This was not even a disagreement. This was plain, ordinary, everyday talk, which consisted quite simply of contradicting everything anyone else had to say. Quarreling, on the other hand, was confined to family members only, with the door closed and the windows shut. Then there was shouting, shrieking, crying, verbal insults, and praying to God to punish the heathen who had dared take up residence in this house.

To friends and relatives, however, Mrs. Moreno referred to her husband as a "fine man." For a long period in her life,

31

she dressed only in white as a sign of her favor in the eyes of God, and held prayer meetings in her home that neighbors whispered about.

"What do you *do* at those meetings?" teachers asked the young Ted, as rumors made the rounds.

"Pray," Ted would whisper, which did not quite explain the outbursts of religious fervor that he witnessed from the doorway, the shaking and babbling.

As the Morenos grew older, however, and life around them became more sophisticated, they retired to the privacy of their little house with its "No Trespassing" sign at the driveway. And by the time my own family moved into the neighborhood, few knew much at all about the elderly couple who lived to themselves on a back lot.

In December, nine months before our wedding, Ted wrote his last letter to me from the University:

> My leaving school at the end of this quarter is practically certain. That means getting a job, preferably a rough one that doesn't involve much mental work. Leaving school and working for at least a year will be an opportunity for me to do many of the things I've wanted to do for a long time. . . .

And so he left, with four years of English literature behind him, and took a job with a construction company in Oakton, spreading hot tar. He wanted to earn money to start our marriage, to get away from the academic life temporarily, to mix with people, to know himself. He came back to his parents' home to live meanwhile. And because he was ambivalent about leaving school, he commuted to the Big City once a week for sessions with a sympathetic psychoanalyst to receive support in his decision. It all seemed so perfectly sensible, so well-planned. . . .

Didn't the Morenos frighten me? Didn't Ted's background give me pause, sound an alarm, make me wary? No. Seventeen is the time when life is eminently conquerable. There is no disadvantage, ill fortune, or tragedy that can stop us. We can overcome evil with good, be kind to those who despise us, and cast off both our heredity and environment with the simple statement, "I don't want to be like that, therefore I won't."

As the months passed and the wedding date grew closer, Ted grew more and more estranged from his parents and no longer took me to his house. His mother sent me a necklace for my eighteenth birthday, "to match your eyes," but told Ted that it was too bad there was something wrong with my nose that kept me from being pretty. She was not sure I was the girl for him, was afraid I lacked maturity. When we met on the street, she and I, she complained that she did not see much of me anymore, or her son either, for that matter. And she felt that in some stealthy way, that psychiatrist was turning Ted against them, didn't I agree?

It was a difficult time. I longed for in-laws I could confide in, but Ted insisted they know as little as possible of our plans, determined that we would live our own lives. He bought his first car to the derision of his father who felt he should have been consulted ("Whoever hear of Studebaker?"). The more Ted cooled toward his parents, the more they struggled for control, and Ted insisted that his mother would have her nose under the covers on our wedding night if we'd let her. (She was invited to two of my bridal showers and presented me with a bedspread at one, a pink nightgown at another. Ted would not let me use either.)

My own parents did not really approve of the match. They worried about the disparity of our backgrounds, our ages, our educations. My mother tried hard to be my confidante, and I enjoyed this intimacy. But it did not stop the wedding. Ted was already a part of the family. He found the atmosphere in our home soothing, if not particularly stimulating.

We were not an especially close family who stood up for

each other, right or wrong. There was no special pride in ourselves as a group. But we did not shout or attack each other verbally. We did not distort or contradict. Love was expressed through concern for each other more than enjoyment of mutual pleasures. Once the childhood bickering had passed, we became a group of five individuals who went our separate ways in politeness, and Ted wanted to belong.

The wedding took place on a Gilbert and Sullivan set, directed by the Marx Brothers. The church organist was miffed because Ted had directed her to play Handel's *Water Music* instead of her beloved Liszt. I was so used to wearing my sister's discards, that I walked down the aisle in her wedding dress, which I hated. At the last moment Ted decided not to kiss me in front of the congregation and, after an awkward pause, escorted me back to the foyer where we stood beside, but a yard away from, the Morenos—a real feat, considering the fact that Ted and his parents were scarcely speaking. Mrs. M. wore a dress of deep blue (for mourning?) and Mr. Moreno wore his frozen, patented smile, which gave his face the appearance of old leather almost ready to crack. They joshed with me, laughed with friends and neighbors, trying desperately to produce some sort of reconciliation—recognition, even—from Ted.

After a reception in the church basement, I went home to change and pack. Exit the happy couple. Ted had decided we could do without the tin cans and old shoes, and to insure that the wedding day would be a thing of beauty, we would simply slip quietly out the door with my monstrous Samsonite suitcase and walk the block to his house where we would get unobtrusively into the Studebaker and drive off into the sunset.

As it turned out, there was a crowd of two dozen relatives waiting when we emerged with the Samsonite, and when it appeared we were merely going around the corner for our honeymoon, they all decided to come along, carrying their signs and tin cans with them. We even picked up some neighborhood kids and a couple of dogs for the procession. In a shower of rice, with aunts, uncles, and cousins in tow, we walked up the driveway marked "No Trespassing," past the house where the elder Morenos stood on their front porch gawking, and over to the garage, where we found the door, of course, padlocked. As his parting words to his father, Ted had to ask for the key. The Patriarch made a production of giving it to him, and the Gilbert and Sullivan chorus surged into the garage to decorate the car. We were three miles out of town when I remembered I had forgotten the jackets and coat in my closet, and Ted said we weren't going back for anything in the world. Consequently I froze the entire time.

We headed for a neighboring state in exhausted silence, but I decided I didn't care. Hadn't he promised that I would never mind the cold after we were married, or even feel it then?

For one year, we had been promising each other the moon once we were married. We pledged devotion, passion, and happiness sublime. "After we're married" became the zenith of all our dreams, the fulfillment of all our cravings. If we could just be alone together forever, away from the world, everything would be all right. And now we were married, we were legal, and we were alone. Bring on the joy!

I was a virgin, which was not so unusual then for a girl of eighteen. But Ted was a virgin also, and what one of us lacked in experience and expertise, the other matched measure for measure.

As some girls dream of a long white gown and veil, I dreamed of sex. I fantasied it, craved it, and felt that a woman penetrated was a woman fulfilled. I longed to face the world the next day as a woman who had been had, and was sure

35

that everyone would know it by the dreamy look in my eyes, the smile on my lips, a certain aura that spelled s-e-x. I was dismayed then, when Ted said on our way to the border that —what with all the tension of the day—it might be better to wait until we were feeling more relaxed.

Wait? I, with the sheer white nightgown and the contraceptive foam? I, who had counted the months, weeks, days and hours when we would be locked in each other's arms, belly to belly?

For the next two hours I concentrated on proving how relaxed I was. I stayed completely loose and unruffled when Ted pulled out the map (our route marked meticulously in red) and announced that we would reach our destination much later than he'd expected. I stayed calm and collected when he turned down at least a half dozen motels as being unsuitable somehow. And when at last we took a "honeymoon" cottage with two (!) double beds because it was all that was left, I said absolutely nothing against it. There was even a plywood rainbow over the driveway to suggest we would soon discover our pot of gold. Ted parked the Studebaker beneath it and took the Samsonite inside.

The cottage had been shut up and smelled of stale tobacco. The owner hung around to explain that if we used both double beds we would be charged extra, then made a few jokes and disappeared. We remembered we had had no dinner, and had nothing edible along except a single slice of wedding cake and some Spearmint gum. We were tired, tense, and strangely untalkative, despite my pretenses.

How could it be that we had embraced every chance we could get in my parents' living room, yet stood here calmly, alone, hanging up clothes? In place of Brahms and Schubert, we had the drone of a ventilating fan. In place of candles, we had a Gideon Bible. In place of wine and roses, we had two double beds and a table covered with oilcloth. It was not the right mood for sex, but I wanted it anyway.

While Ted changed into pajamas, I washed off all my make-up in the bathroom and carefully put it all on again. I checked my toenails to see that they were clean, and made sure that my navel was free of lint. Then I used the small plunger to apply the contraceptive foam, compliments of Planned Parenthood, put on the white gown which was two sizes too large (the only one I could find that was suitably sheer) and entered the bedroom. Ta da!

Ted was already in bed, and I came on with all the modesty of a Mack truck. I proceeded to snuggle up against him, entwining my legs in his, determined not to remain a virgin a minute longer than necessary.

The fact that my defloration took place three nights hence was not Ted's fault, but mine. After our first few clumsy attempts, I was certain that we simply weren't doing it right. I had dismissed all rumors of pain as old wives' tales from terrified women. The fact that it hurt when Ted tried to push inside me was simply evidence that we hadn't quite got the hang of it, and we gave up quickly lest it traumatize us.

But inwardly I was coming unglued. I had visions of carting ourselves off to the family doctor and performing my defloration on his examining table. How did people do it, anyway? Did they use mirrors, or what? I was disappointed, anxious, desperate. During the day, people smiled at us and asked if we were enjoying married life, and we smiled back and gave all the right answers, but all the while I was dying inside. We weren't husband and wife at all, simply kids who made a nightly ritual of mauling each other before giving up and going reluctantly to sleep.

On the fourth night, Ted convinced me that the pain was inevitable, and because there was nothing left to do, I agreed

37

to try again. This time he did not stop when I cried out, but pushed against me harder and harder. I found myself shoving at his shoulders to hold him off, but he broke through the hymen and pushed himself in.

The pain was beyond belief. I have never felt such a pain since, not even in childbirth—a sudden, ripping pain that seemed to cut me wide open and made me scream. The sheets looked like the floor of a slaughterhouse. Not only had I bled profusely, but the shock had brought on my menstrual period two weeks early. I made my way to the bathroom with blood streaming down my legs, and Ted followed, dropping to his knees and kissing my stomach, begging me to bleed on him, a scene straight out of William Faulkner. I was a woman at last, and it hurt like anything.

I could scarcely walk the next day and could sit only with the greatest care. At the end of the week, we headed south in the Studebaker to an apartment of our own, hopeful that sex would get better, problems easier, and love stronger. We would still have the perfect marriage that Van de Velde talked about—once we got organized.

Some men are born cerebral and, like those who are left-handed, should remain so all their lives. Perhaps shifting the focus to muscles and sinews causes kinks in the central nervous system that multiply into madness. Perhaps the shock of leaving the ivy-covered walls of the University, where pale-faced students talked Aristotle, and entering the land of the hard hat, where red-necked men talked cunt, triggered an irreversible process. Perhaps Ted knew, sitting beside them at lunchtime as they ate their thick bologna sandwiches and examined each passing woman as though she were spread-eagled before them, that this was a world he could never enter, even though it was all around him.

The worst discovery was that, having left his books in order to get to know people, he didn't really like them after all. They could not be underlined, categorized, subdivided, and indexed. There were variables, nuances, subtleties, and inconsistencies he hadn't reckoned with, and they, unlike the characters in *Vanity Fair,* never stayed in the outline he had made for them.

The beefy men in sweat-soaked shirts were not quite what Ted had in mind when he envisioned men of the earth. Their jokes were different from those he heard in the University washrooms, different even from those of the Air Force officers that he heard in the barracks. As Ted described them, the men on the construction crew had tufts of hair growing out their nostrils and from the crevices of their ears, and to a man they reeked of BO. They rammed their huge hands between each other's legs and grabbed at genitals. They compared the food in their lunch boxes to feces and clots of menstrual blood. The only adjectives they used were expletives, and they especially resented the newcomer in their midst who listened from the sidelines.

We settled down in a three-room apartment in our home town, and Ted traded his job on the construction crew for a place on an assembly line. I took a job as locker-room attendant in the YWCA, where I gave out keys to society women who came to reduce in the mornings, and to ponytailed schoolgirls who came to swim in the afternoons. Except for the spectacle of two lesbians who occasionally grappled together suggestively on the locker-room floor, and the unsought advice of the cleaning woman who suggested douching with lemon juice to prevent conception, I was bored in this windowless room, and retreated to my notebook where I could write uninterrupted during the slow hours, surrounded on all sides by the smell of chlorine and wet towels.

January came, and Ted was still unsettled in his plans. We decided that I should go to the local junior college till he felt ready to return to the University for a degree in education. And so I enrolled—the only married woman in the school.

Who can describe the early years of a marriage? Some days were love and bliss, and some were hell on earth. Life was a mixture of laughter, fun, and crying jags (mine). There were tender words and devastating criticism (his)—gentleness, concern, and also sarcasm. The college man with the quiet voice and soft sweaters was replaced more often than not by a cynical accountant of human frailties, and the young bride, who was trying so hard to be mature, collapsed like a folding chair at the very hint of disagreement.

Between the bouts of lectures and tears, however, there were exquisite moments that were a delight to both of us. Coming from a home where affection was expressed primarily by tone of voice and a certain look in the eyes, where kisses and hugs were reserved for arriving and departing, I found it new and wonderful that I could caress Ted, fondle him, stroke his cheeks and forehead or kiss his eyelids, and Ted in turn found it possible, though difficult at first, to respond. There were many times, when we lay together on the couch just holding and stroking each other, that Ted would laugh aloud with the sheer pleasure of it, and would tell me that I had changed his whole life. I was incredibly happy to hear it. What more could I possibly want?

As far as misconceptions about the matrimonial state, you name it, I had it. Maturity, I believed, was self-control. Period. The superwoman was infinitely patient, never raised her voice—beareth all things, believeth all things, hopeth all things, and endureth. Charity Sublime, that was me. But inevitably sexy. The mature woman, as I saw her, was a model of patience and control in the daylight hours, and wildly impatient in the bedroom. Like a werewolf making the change when the moon was full, I thought I could easily shift from

40

complete submission in our day-to-day relationship to earthy orgasms once we reached the bedroom.

On the other hand, I expected the same amount of patience from Ted, and was dismayed to find him so intolerant. The first dinner I prepared was worse than a disaster—it was a living, mucky stench. Ted was hungry, not amused. When I tried to save on the laundry bill by washing clothes in the bathtub and they all turned gray, he was disgusted, not grateful. And when, on our first anniversary, he returned home hot, grease-stained, and bone-tired and found me dressed in my wedding gown with all the candles lit, he wanted only a shower and a cold drink, not me.

The first two years of marriage found me frequently hurt and Ted habitually irritated. He seemed resentful that I had been able to go back to school while he marked time in a factory, even though it was of his own choosing. And so the marriage finally took a turn for the better when I got my diploma and we headed back to the Big Town.

In a strange turnabout, Ted decided to enter the business world temporarily. He took a job as a medical underwriter for an insurance company, bought several smart, conservative suits, enrolled for night school courses at a technological institute, working on a master's degree in mathematics, and continued his project of educating me on the side. I took a job as clinical secretary in the University hospital, enrolled in correspondence courses for college credit, and continued to write. Life was busy, full, and quite manageable.

Our relationship could best be described as professor–student, lecturer–listener, master–subject. Ted was an enthusiastic live-in tutor, and the marriage a sixteen-hour-a-day adventure in education. When I failed to meet his expectations, however—when my interpretation of a poem, for example, fell far short of profundity, which was often—his criticism was scathing. There were times I could do nothing right, and then my errors simply snowballed. I could not talk to his friends, it seemed, or give our address, or fill out an application for stack privileges without embarrassing him. I was shallow, he said, self-conscious, semi-illiterate, and was abominably ignorant of music. I was immature, unpolished, unsophisticated, and, what's more, my birthmark was ugly.

I had little confidence in myself when we married, and after two years of marriage, even less. Because Ted seemed disgusted or embarrassed or both if I walked through the room naked, I learned soon enough to stay clothed. Even underthings upset him, being transparent. The only thing worse than my mind, it seemed, was my body.

The remarkable, amazing, astounding fact was that I believed everything Ted said, as though his opinions were, indeed, fact. If Ted said that I was semi-illiterate or that my backside was ugly, then—God's truth—it was so. If he praised the psychoanalytic theories of Jung and Adler one day and vilified them the next, I nodded my woolly head and baaed out my agreement. Much as I worshiped his *Harvard Classics,* which took up an entire bookcase in our living room, I did not bat an eye when he suddenly labeled them pretentious and sold them to an ecstatic bookdealer for scarcely anything at all. And if he had rushed down again to buy them himself the following day, I would probably have gone along and carried them home on my back.

It was not as though I were entirely without merit, however. Way down in my heart of hearts, where people know much more than they know that they know, I realized there was a strength that Ted had overlooked. I made friends among the doctors and nurses in the University clinic and found an acceptance I did not get at home. I even tried out for the esteemed University choir, and was admitted, enduring the director's hysterical tantrums in which he shouted at me

42

in Italian because of my name and flung his music over the edge of the balcony if the tenors came in one measure too soon. I continued to write and sell short stories to magazines no one had ever heard of before, and though Ted insisted I had the sort of talent that enabled me to write eleven pages on absolutely nothing, he could not explain the checks that came from time to time.

If I was punished by sarcasm and criticism, though, I was rewarded with a world I had never known before. Weekends were spent attending lectures and art shows, or Mozart operas in the park. Having been raised on Greer Garson and Hedy Lamarr, I fell in love with the movies *Bicycle Thief, La Strada,* and *Gold of Naples.* In Oakton, we had gone to the Young Couples' parties where we played parlor games and discussed meat loaf. Now we went places where people in African togas lounged about talking psychoanalysis and existentialism. We bought bicycles and explored old streets, picnicked at the beaches, and discovered small neighborhood restaurants that only the University students seemed to know. I was, in short, being demolished and reconstructed simultaneously, and each session with my mentor was like being on the witness stand before an impatient prosecutor:

Why did I believe what I'd read in *Time*? Who was the reporter? What were his sources?

As for the editorial in the newspaper, what could be said on the opposite side? If a story contained only half-truths, wasn't the whole piece a falsehood?

Why did I speak in generalities when there were exceptions to everything?

What were the subconscious reasons for wanting what I did, fearing what I did, avoiding what I did?

How had I arrived at my political beliefs? My morals? Where did I get my concept of God?

My private education began with Thackeray's *Vanity Fair,* followed by several books by Dickens, *War and Peace,* Shakespeare's plays, and the collected works of Sigmund Freud. In the evenings, after dinner, we would open our studio couch and lie there reading to each other from Balzac, Butler, or George Santayana. Ted read *The Canterbury Tales* to me, taught me to pronounce Chaucerian English, and together we would recite:

> Whan that Aprille with his shoures sote
> The droghte of Marche hath perced to the rote,
> And bathed every veyne in swich licour,
> Of which vertu engendred is the flour . . .

For several months I was put on a steady diet of nineteenth-century continental novels by Dostoevski, Flaubert, Tolstoi, and Zola. Then, in a direct about-face, I concentrated on Sinclair Lewis, Upton Sinclair, John Steinbeck, and Faulkner, whom I adored.

We listened to our beloved FM station, featuring BBC productions, sociological dramas, poetry readings, and Studs Terkel interviewing the folk musicians of the day on a program called *The Midnight Special.* Ted introduced me to Hayakawa's *Language in Action,* Sumner's *Folkways,* and Frazier's *Golden Bough.* We read books on the sex lives of the apes and the rituals of the Samoans. We debated *The Heathens* and *Religion Without Revelation,* Bertrand Russell and Erich Fromm. Everyone I met seemed so much more secure and sophisticated than I was, and I struggled for this marvelous store of knowledge that I hoped would reward me with self-confidence and everything nice.

And then, of course, there was music. Ted explained that the best way to listen was simply to put on a record and go about my work, repeating it once each day until I found myself knowing little bits and pieces. At random I chose Mozart's *Jupiter* Symphony. On the third playing, it began to make sense. I was remembering wisps of melodies, cadences, and rolling crescendoes. I played it constantly, eagerly awaiting the familiar passages, feeling them approach as hungrily as one awaits an orgasm, glorying in music that grew richer each time it was heard, so full of meaning and depth that it would take an eternity, it seemed, to learn all its secrets.

Then it was Mozart's thirty-ninth and fortieth, Brahms' first three symphonies, Bach's *Brandenburg Concertos,* and Beethoven's Seventh. Slowly I learned the difference between the romantic, classical, and baroque. Ted taught me where Scarlatti came in, as well as Schubert and Berlioz. He delighted in playing unknown pieces and teaching me to recognize the period in which they were written. We got the libretto to *Così fan tutte* and sang it to each other. We became adept at warbling Handel arias and outdid each other singing the *Messiah*:

> The pe-e-ople that wa-a-lked,
> in da-aa-aa-aa-aa-ark-ness,
> That wa-a-lked in da-aa-aa-aa-aa-ark-ness,
> The pe-e-ople that wa-a-lked,
> That wa-lked in dark-ness,
> Have se-en a great light.

We spent Saturday mornings in the Disc Shop, secluded in the little glass-walled booths, listening to the same symphony by four different orchestras before we made our choice. We surrounded ourselves with good recordings, good books, good prints, and I found happiness in these, if not in myself. The final step in my education was a stint in psychotherapy, to gain the same insights into myself that Ted felt he had gained from his own. I went eagerly, for problems both real and imagined, glad that at last I had a confidant. Though the doctor spoke in heavy Hungarian accents, and I often could not even understand what he said, he was someone who would listen to my side of the story, would accept what I felt, and who did not seem to feel, as Ted had felt, that I was in such urgent need of an overhaul.

The world was growing wider and wider.

> In the room the women come and go
> Talking of Michelangelo . . .

What did Eliot mean? Ted prodded. Why did this appear twice in the same poem? Did it portray shallowness? Superficiality? Think again. . . .

There were times I did not care—times when Ted too heavily permeated the thing itself—when I could not read a poem without hearing his voice reciting it precisely, when I could not hear a record without imagining the compulsive tap of his fingers on the bookstand, keeping time. There were occasions I shut myself off from it all and wrote instead, and was able to escape so thoroughly that I always felt refreshed when I came back, though I'd never left the room.

The more I read, the more I discovered there was to read. The more I knew, the more I discovered I didn't know. Where once I had assumed that Ted and his psychiatrist together represented the pinnacle of knowledge, they had now begun to shrink in size—if only a centimeter—and the University along with them. At the same time Ted was teaching me to think by questioning my values, challenging my ideas, and criticizing my opinions, he was teaching me, probably unaware, to question his.

But I was teaching Ted something also: to laugh. Always so serious, he seemed almost to have to be taught, and I found delight in saying something in just the right way to bring about that quick spasm of laughter, surprising even himself. I began to feel that he did, perhaps, need me after all, more than he realized.

He was destined, like Gallia, to be divided into parts. Whatever he chose gratified one segment of himself and antagonized another. He was doomed, it seemed, to be perpetually at odds with himself—the battle of yin and yang, masculine and feminine, aggressive and passive, intellectual and social. Compromise, for some reason, was out of the question. The components of his body chemistry refused to blend. He was doomed if he succeeded and doomed if he didn't.

In some ways, however, this was the healthiest period of his life. He had gained fifteen pounds and the conservative suits were replaced by a larger size with a little more flair. He proved to be an excellent medical underwriter and was offered both a promotion and a raise, but he refused, causing shock waves in the corporate management. Why did he refuse? Because he would be committing himself to the business world versus the intellectual, he told me. Was that so bad? Yes, there was a Ph.D. in his future. Why couldn't he graciously accept the raise and promotion anyway? Surely none of the other employees felt committed to pledge themselves to the company for life. Because he felt he would be selling himself down the river, he said. The refusal held, he continued working at his original starting pay, and his supervisor had considerable difficulty writing up the report.

Ted completed the work for a master's degree in mathematics at the technological institute and, in another surprise move, invited his father—who had since retired to New Mexico with the Good Woman—to attend the graduation ceremony. But not his mother. Mr. Moreno came alone.

It was our best visit together as relatives. Mr. M. arrived

in his wide-brimmed hat and Truman smile and, still puzzled about the invitation, tried his best to be pleasant—patriarchal and dogmatic, true, but pleasant. He stayed at a hotel but came to our efficiency apartment each day for meals. We took pictures of each other in the park, joked, saw the sights of the city in the Studebaker he had said wouldn't last six months, and patronized the local delicatessen for things that Mr. M. couldn't live without. At the graduation ceremony, he was upset briefly that Ted had dropped the "junior" from his name, but recovered in time to wish Ted well, and gave us a check for a thousand dollars as a graduation gift. More remarkable still, Ted accepted.

On our last night together, Mr. M. took us to an Italian restaurant and played the part of the Godfather, advising us, ordering for us, snapping his fingers at the waiters, and conversing in Italian with everyone who came in. I loved it. Ted tolerated it. And Mr. M. went back to New Mexico the next day well pleased, convinced that the long cold spell was over. I thought the same thing. Perhaps, as Ted was more successful in things that mattered to him, his parents' hold on him would lessen and he would eventually feel threatened no longer. The time would come, I thought, when he would be able to invite his mother as well, and though Ted did not respond when I suggested it, I felt that in time we would all get on reasonably well together. Albuquerque was, after all, a long way from us.

What I had been doing all this time—ever since we married, in fact—was making myself worthy of Ted. Each day I took a few books to work and studied after the last patient had been seen. I taught myself the touch system on the clinic's typewriter. I spent my lunch hour in the library, practiced the *St. John Passion* with the University choir, and—while Ted spent the evenings studying—went to my analyst twice a week and spent the rest of the time writing a virtual tidal wave of stories. Partly it was an escape from my work, for if there was one job in the whole world I should never have taken, it was anything to do with a hospital.

There are objective people and there are subjective people, and as subjective people go, I was the most suggestible. If a patient's X-rays showed a shadow on the lung, I soon found it difficult to breathe. If there was a diagnosis of brain tumor, I developed pain at the back of my head. If there was a report of cancer of the colon, I felt twitches and tremors over my entire abdomen, and for two years I lived with the firm belief that any morning I was going to awaken to find that telltale lump on the side of my neck or on the back of my knee or somewhere down in the groin.

I did not just feel sorry for the patients who came to the clinic, I lived their lives. Because it was my job to check the charts before each patient's visit—to read the diagnosis, see that the tests which were ordered were reported in full—I was one of the first to see the evidence that would either confirm or refute the doctor's diagnosis. I would know that at two o'clock a young, vivacious woman was going to come into the waiting room smiling, as she always did, relieved that the tests were over, confident that she would get an answer and the medicine she felt she needed. When she came I would sit woodenly at my desk, sorting through papers as she went inside, staring out at her husband and children who were reading magazines on the couch. And forty minutes later I would see her come out of the conference room with the doctor, her face drained of color. I would see the husband rise to meet them, and watch as they stepped discreetly around the corner, away from the children, for a conversation in low tones. I would feel the strength and the hope oozing out of my own pores as I caught the shock and terror on their faces. Some day it would be me—some day it would be all of us.

When Ted was admitted to graduate school, I decided I did not want to spend the next two or three years looking for tumors in my armpits. I wanted a change, but I had completed only one more year of college, and three would get me nowhere. As a first small step toward independence, I sang the final note of the *St. John Passion* with the Chapel Choir, then turned in my robe and music and walked out on the director who had made me so miserable. And I applied for a state test that would enable me to teach school on a limited certificate if I passed.

Then Ted's fears began. I went to work each morning to instruct patients about proctoscopies and returned home at night to a husband who was checking the curtain rods for concealed microphones. During the day I arranged appointments for radiation therapy for advanced metastases, and in the evening I watched Ted pace from one window to the next, looking for Dr. Gerber out there on the roof somewhere. Between nine and five I listened to patients tell horror stories of how their moles had grown larger until the cancerous roots had spread throughout their bodies, and at night I listened to Ted's accusations that my birthmark was the sign of Cain and the cause of all his troubles—my birthmark and my nakedness and my menstrual blood and all my womanness. One day I stepped in the minor operating room to give a message to one of the doctors and was horrified to see them lift half a man's face—a plastic front—from his head. The rest had been eaten away by cancer, yet still this remains of a man could moan—this man without eyes, nose, or mouth was alive, and came in periodically to have his face removed and the inside of his head tinkered with. And that night I went home to find that the terrors of my own household were now being verbalized. The Communists, Ted said, were planning to kill him because their leader wanted to marry me.

It was nice, in a way, to be wanted after doubting it these

last five years. It was nice, after believing so long that I was undesirable, to think that anyone would go to such lengths to possess me. It was great to know that after all the sarcasm and criticism of my intellectual abilities, Ted was actually concerned about losing me. But it was obvious now beyond any doubt that he had been more sick than I had imagined. I urged him to return to his psychiatrist, but he refused.

I told my own psychiatrist, but he did not really believe me. It was too farfetched. Ted must be kidding me. He was still going to school, wasn't he, still studying, still hard at work on his assistantship? Was I, perhaps, given to exaggeration?

Ted had already decided to leave the University at the end of the quarter. It was all a mistake, he said. He should have stayed in business. It was all right with me. I thought that once he was away from the source of his fears, however irrational, he could look at them objectively and then I could persuade him to see his former analyst, Dr. Pollard, again. I didn't care about his Ph.D. and it seemed more evident than ever that it was his mother's dreams for him, more than his father's, that were driving him mad. Time, I believed, would force him to take some kind of action to help himself. And so I told no one else, because I could not imagine how anyone could help. What could his parents do out in New Mexico but worry? How do you tell someone that your husband is out of his mind?

Dear Mother:
   We are having a beautiful autumn, and have been enjoying University life except for the Communists, who keep climbing the fire escape at night, which is why Ted keeps a cupboard pushed against the back door. . . .

Dear Fran:
   I'm sorry I haven't written sooner, but it's been a hectic fall. As you know, Ted was accepted for graduate work at the Uni-

51

versity, but we don't go out much because he believes someone is trying to gun him down. . . .

Dear Paul:
    The reason I'm writing instead of Ted is because he's been busy planting suicide notes in his pants cuff. . . .

Dear Mom and Dad Moreno:
    I'm sorry to have to write that after graduating from the Technological Institute and entering the University, your son has gone absolutely mad, and there's not a thing you can do about it. . . .

The fact was that I could do nothing about it either. I had passed my teaching exam and was ready to make a change in my own life, but it seemed the worst possible time. By January, my description of Ted's behavior had finally begun to alarm my psychiatrist, and he felt that Ted should be persuaded to return to his own doctor. But he had no suggestions for doing so. Finally, I took a day off work and rode the train out to the eastern suburbs to apply for a teaching job. I was hired by a superintendent in a small town and gave two weeks' notice at the hospital.

"Why leave now? You just got a raise," they said. "What could be worse than a classroom full of noisy children?"

Carcinoma of the liver, cancer of the stomach, and endless recitations on the collection of stool specimens.

"It's more convenient for you here. Your husband can drop you off on the way to classes."

My husband is home disassembling the toilet, looking for microphones. There will be no more classes for him.

The fact that my life was going ahead and his was coming to a standstill agitated Ted even further. He did not say so directly, but he seemed hurt, as though my ability to keep my head above water, however feebly, kept us apart somehow—as though he would find more comfort in my sinking along with him. He did not eat, but spent the time striding tensely around the apartment.

And then, suddenly, he announced that he was going to New Mexico briefly for a reconciliation with his parents, and invited me to come.

Why didn't I greet the announcement with joy and jubilation? Why didn't I think that a reconciliation might heal all wounds, solve his conflicts, yin the yang, and give Ted a glorious shove toward maturity, with the past forgiven and the future his, to do with as he liked?

Had it been any other time, when Ted was strong and self-confident, I would have welcomed the opportunity. I would have lovingly purchased gifts for my in-laws and set out determined to be the dutiful, understanding daughter-in-law. Instead, the prospect of Ted's returning to his parents like a small, frightened child appalled me. I remembered the Fine Man and the Good Woman at their worst, and wondered what would happen to Ted if they quarreled over him now. Instinct for survival, I suppose, but I told Ted I would stay and he could go alone. I had just given notice at the clinic, and could hardly leave immediately, before they'd found someone to take my place.

Whenever I think of Ted now, I remember him as he looked at the train window when it left the station. He had wired his parents that he was coming, and, as the train pulled slowly away, I noticed the dark hollows around his eyes. He had kissed me good-bye as though he never expected to see me again, and through the dusty glass of the train window, I saw there were tears on his cheeks.

I love you, he mouthed silently, and continued staring at me intently as the train went on.

I took a bus back to our apartment and realized that it was the first night we had been apart since we'd married five years before. In fact, I was twenty-three, and it was the first time I had been alone in a house in my life. From the time I was born till age eighteen, my parents had been there to make the major decisions for me, and after I married, Ted took over the responsibilities. If there wasn't a man to knock on my bedroom door and ask if I wanted a ride to school, there was a man to snuggle up to at night.

A man. The very word held the connotation of something marvelous, much to be desired. That there were also corpulent men, smelly men, revolting, disgusting, crude men seemed irrelevant somehow. To be so attractive that a *man* would want to spend his life with me had always been an unspoken hope. To fail was to be nothing, for a woman without a man was pathetic.

Why? I did not know.

Was a man without a woman equally pathetic? Of course not. Because then it was by choice.

And could not a woman also choose to be single? Why on earth would she want to? Who would not want this badge, this proof of desirability, this *man*—to be worn around the shoulders like a security blanket?

Where did I get such ideas? All I knew was that it was imperative to keep my husband, psychotic or not, because I had little image of self apart from him. We were a couple, a partnership, a marriage. If anything happened to me, he, of course, would marry again. If anything happened to him, I would come apart at the seams. It seemed a perfectly logical assumption.

And now suddenly I was really alone. It was very strange, very lonely, but not entirely unpleasant. I was surprised. I got up and dressed without anyone reminding me to hurry. I ate breakfast and read the paper without anyone interrupting me to read aloud sections of the editorial page. I walked to work on my own two legs and came home to eat whatever I alone wanted for dinner. I spent the first two evenings writing, pouring out my imaginary comings and goings, losing myself on the scribbled page. Most of all, Ted and his problems were temporarily gone. The fears had gone with him. The apartment was blissfully quiet.

On the third day, I received a phone call at work from Mr. Moreno. His voice was slow and deliberate, speaking precisely as though keeping an iron grip on his rage, valiantly masking the pain. Ted, Jr., was in the hospital, he said, and wanted me to come at once. He had arrived in Albuquerque sick and confused, convinced that he was covered with invisible poisoned powder. There was a pause, and then the words came out in a torrent. It had been only six months since he had visited us, and Ted had been in the best of spirits and good health. What on earth, his inflection implied, had I done to their son?

I was overcome with guilt. I could never do anything right. This proved it. Why hadn't I gone with Ted as he'd asked? Why hadn't I told his parents sooner? Why hadn't I called Ted's psychiatrist and had him committed to a hospital? Now there were twelve hundred miles between us, and Ted wanted me to come.

It never for a moment occurred to me not to go. I told my supervisor at the hospital that my husband had gone out West to visit his parents and had been hospitalized with peritonitis. I had to leave at once. One thing about working in a hospital, you learn some marvelous names for excuses.

At home, I packed a suitcase—the old Samsonite that weighed twenty pounds unpacked—and took the bus to the train station because I hadn't the slightest idea how one goes about getting on a plane. I may have known about Schopenhauer and Schubert, but I knew very little about the practical world. Not only did I not know how to get a

55

flight to Albuquerque, I couldn't even get the right train. I assumed that if I got on the first to leave the station, I would reach New Mexico sooner, so I found myself on a mail train that stopped at every town of over five hundred people —a three-day trip in a coach seat. I knew nothing about reserving a bed.

I did not sleep more than an hour or two each night. Mornings and afternoons were a haze of blurred depots, trees, and scruffy fields as seen through the dirty window. Nights were an exercise in torture as I curled myself in the fetal position and tried to fit on the coach seat. I dreamed always that I was stretching my legs, and after the second night, I craved nothing as desperately as a full-length bed.

An hour before we reached Albuquerque, I went to the women's lounge to clean up. It was a room-sized compartment with a sink, a dressing table, and a couch. I had stripped completely to take a sponge bath—my first in three days— glad that the train had stopped so I could keep my balance while I washed my feet. There was a tap on the window, and I whirled around to discover that the blind did not quite reach the bottom of the sill. In that quarter inch of exposed glass, a group of soldiers outside were leering and laughing. Pigs.

As the train pulled into the station at Albuquerque, I tried to brace myself for in-laws with murder on their minds. I was semicomatose from lack of sleep, and wouldn't even have Ted there to defend me. I did not know the city, the bus lines, or even which hospital Ted was in. I was completely dependent on his parents, and would see them now as they really were.

The sun was hot. I had left the Midwest in four inches of snow and sweltered now in my wool dress. Not only was I on the lowest percentile in practical living, I was a big fat zero when it came to geography. The Morenos were waiting for me on the platform. They were not only polite, they were very polite. They were soft-spoken and gentle, all tenderness and concern. I was touched.

"I'd like to see Ted," I said after we'd greeted each other.

Later, they told me. First I must want to rest. I must want to change clothes. I must want a nice cool drink . . . to talk.

The heat and fatigue were beginning to take their toll and I felt I was losing my voice. I was fine, I told them, but would like to go right to the hospital and see Ted. Later, they said. We had to wait till visiting hours. Could I call him then, I wondered. No, that wasn't allowed.

Mrs. Moreno got in the back seat of the car, insisting that I sit up front with "Dad" so I could see better. I had a sudden fear that they might kill me—choke me from behind with piano wire. God, I was beginning to think like Ted. His madness was contagious.

Mr. Moreno must have driven fifteen miles to go five. He took the longest, most complicated route possible to get to their house, showing me the distant hills, flower gardens, library, University—especially the University. It was a bloody guided tour! I got the history of New Mexico, the climate, the major industries, imports and exports, and the size of the student body on campus. I got a long recitation of Albuquerque's cultural highlights, a list of all the artists who had appeared in concert over the last two years, and a tour of the churches.

"I want to see Ted!" I said finally, my voice breaking.

"She wants to see Ted," Mrs. Moreno repeated from the back seat, as though remembering suddenly what I'd come twelve hundred miles for.

There were still forty minutes to go till visting hours once we'd reached the house, so I agreed at least to sit down for a lemonade. I noticed the Morenos taking chairs directly across from me, one on either side, as though it were pre-arranged. Then I got the commercial.

Mr. Moreno said he had a proposition to make. Mrs. Moreno interrupted to say that it wasn't really a proposition, just a vagrant thought that had suddenly occurred to them, and after arguing for several minutes more over which of them was going to spring it on me, Mr. M. got the upper hand: they would pay for all of Ted's medical expenses, put me through the University, and buy us a house if I would just agree to move to Albuquerque so they could have their son near them. Did I want more? Just name it. Something else they hadn't mentioned? All I had to do was give in.

"I want to see Ted," I said, and stood up. We went out to the car.

I tried to keep my wits about me on the way to the hospital. I told them I had just been hired for a third-grade classroom. I said that I didn't really have anything against New Mexico, but I didn't feel we should make such an important move while Ted was in his present mental state —that after he recovered, he and I together could decide where we should live. Besides, we had all of our friends back home—our whole way of life. They replied that evidently neither our friends nor our way of life had helped Ted in the least, and I was in no position to argue.

At the hospital, there was the first glimmer of hope when the nurse said that we could visit Ted only one at a time. The Morenos graciously told me that I could go first. At least I would be able to ask Ted questions without them there to answer for him.

Ted looked considerably better than he had when he left home. His color was better, and he was relieved when I came in.

"I want to go back," he said at once, and took my hand.

58

"It was a mistake for me to come here. I want to go back and see Dr. Pollard and put my head together."

It was too good to be true. He was affectionate, tender, sorry for all the trouble and inconvenience he had caused me. "Just get me out of here," he said, "and let's go home."

I thought of the Morenos waiting for my half of the hour to be over so they could come in. I thought of the fact that I had just arrived and Ted already wanted to go back. I thought of their proposition and what it meant to them, and wondered vaguely if I would even get out of Albuquerque alive. The nurse suggested I talk it over with Ted's doctor, and the doctor said he wished to see us both together. We sat down in his air-conditioned office, husband in striped pajamas, wife in steaming wool dress, and Dr. Greer laid his cards on the table. Ted, he said to both of us together, was obviously in need of psychiatric help. He had periods of rational thinking and insight into himself, however, which was all in his favor. Dr. Greer said he would discharge Ted on one condition: that we take the first available flight back home, and that Ted agree to enter the VA hospital there. Ted was elated. He promised. He was more like himself than I had seen him for some time. The last few months seemed to be passing before his eyes with great lucidity:

> The pe-e-ople that wa-aa-lked,
> in da-aa-aa-aa-aa-ark-ness
> Have se-en a great light.

By the time we got back to the waiting room, Ted's parents were furious. What was this? Where had we gone? What had I been up to? Where did Ted think he was going? By what authority had I walked in this hospital and taken a patient right out of his bed? Had the doctor gone mad? Ted was in no condition to travel. What had I told the doctor? What had I said to Ted? What kind of stories was I spreading about them? They insisted on their own conference with the doctor, and Dr. Greer held firm. Ted, he said, should go back home and work with his own doctor there.

The Morenos were in a frenzy. I tried to explain that it was Ted's idea, Ted's request, but they believed none of it. Everyone was conspiring against them, they said . . . the hospital, the doctors, the nurses, their very own daughter-in-law. . . . It sounded somehow familiar.

We had to go back to their house to get my suitcase. It was only four in the afternoon and the first available flight left at midnight. With no one saying much to anyone else, we drove back to the Morenos' and I decided to take a shower. Ted was loving and passionate. He wanted to get in the shower with me. He wanted to sing Handel arias while he washed his hair. He wanted to make love in the guest room.

I wanted to get out. I wanted to get to the terminal as fast as we possibly could. While I changed clothes, Ted went to the kitchen, and when I came out he was sitting at the table eating peanuts—bowlful after bowlful—discarding the shells on his mother's neat tablecloth, popping nuts into his mouth by the handful . . . a dozen, two dozen, three dozen . . . a peanut shelling machine, endlessly cracking and eating . . . and now strangely silent. Panic began to rise in me again.

The Morenos, however, were talking plenty. Ted's father was angry, his mother bitter. I hadn't even stayed long enough to see the University, to get to know Albuquerque. Why was I so determined to get their son away from them? All these years Ted had never paid them a visit, and now that he was here, I was taking him away again.

60

I felt that things were closing in on me—that the whole world was mad. Ted sat there eating peanuts with no words at all in my defense—no explanations of his own. It was as though he didn't even hear us. He was mad. The Morenos were mad. Dr. Greer was mad for thinking that I could cope with these three lunatics myself until midnight, the magic hour when we would ride off into the darkness.

I sat across the table from Ted and watched his parents pacing restlessly. What hopes they had held for this son of theirs! How proud Mr. Moreno had been at Ted's graduation! How excited they must have been when Ted wired that he was coming, and how appalled when he stepped off the train. How could I expect them to feel anything but bitter? They did not understand what was happening, but neither did I. We were all heading for outer space in a craft gone haywire, and the first contingent took off at midnight.

All the way to the airport they made low accusations, sarcastic remarks, sullen comments. Ted said absolutely nothing. I tried to keep the talk light. I marveled at the streetlights, marveled at the homes we passed in the darkness, marveled at the airport, deluging them with complimentary remarks about Albuquerque now that we were getting out of it, and all the while Ted sat like a corpse at my side.

Once in the terminal, however, Ted began to get irritated in return. To his father's indignant remarks about psychiatry and the ignorance of doctors, Ted replied that a man who had never been to college at all was hardly in a position to judge.

It had been a long, tense day, and Mr. Moreno was in no mood to be contradicted. As Ted's voice grew louder, so did his own, and finally they were shouting at each other there by the baggage counter while his mother stalked off announcing that she would not listen to this slander any longer. She sat down on a row of plastic chairs at one end of the terminal and began to pray.

Oh God in heaven, I said, *tune her out just this once and listen to me. Let the plane come in early, let us get on board, and let the door be closed before anything else can happen. Please.*

There were no good-byes. The plane came in and we got on board and soon the pilot announced that we would be flying at 19,000 feet. *We have been flying at 19,000 feet for the last four months,* I thought. *We have been circling around over the mouth of hell and nobody knows what to do.*

It was dark in the plane, and I fell asleep sitting up. A half hour later we hit some turbulence and I awoke wondering where I was and who I was with. It did not seem possible I had been to New Mexico already and had left so soon, and my mind did not seem to be functioning.

And then I heard a sarcastic voice beside me say flatly, "This was a mistake. I should have stayed in Albuquerque. They'll be waiting for me back home. They'll have their hired thugs there in the terminal, and you'll turn me over to them. You don't want to, but you can't help yourself. They've drugged you too."

Dear God, I said again, but I doubted He was listening.

THREE

THE BIG CITY was a shock to the nervous system. Albuquerque had been hot, but the three days on the train going out had slowly acclimated my body to the heat. Now I was not prepared for the sheer force of the wind or the foot of snow on the sidewalks. The diatribe which Ted had begun against his parents before we left now shifted its focus to me. Who was I really working for? What were they paying me to betray him? Judas Iscariot in disguise, his own wife. Had I no shame, no honor, no loyalty?

I reminded him of his promise to Dr. Greer that we would go immediately to the veteran's hospital, but Ted would not hear of it. He ordered the cab to take us home. It was early morning and we were both exhausted—Ted from talking, I from listening. We slept till noon and awoke to an even grayer day. Then it began all over again—the watching at the windows, the listening at the door, the search for microphones and messages in the bed sheets, the ceaseless, rambling talk and accusations. . . .

That afternoon, on my way back from shopping, I stopped at the drugstore and made a call to Ted's analyst, forgetting that these fifty-minute men are never available by phone except for ten minutes prior to each hour. An operator informed me that I would have to call back at three-fifty. I slipped out of the apartment again at three-fifty, but Dr. Pollard's line was busy and it stayed busy until four, when an operator came on the line and said I would have to call back at four-fifty. With Ted suspecting the worst from my comings and goings, I went to the drugstore again at four-fifty and this time was connected with the friendly, reassuring voice of Dr. Pollard. I explained Ted's symptoms, and told him all we had been through.

"Tell Ted that you called me because you are concerned about him," he advised. "Tell him I suggested that he call me himself and set up an appointment." Then, probably because I sounded so frantic, he added what I'm sure he has regretted ever since: "I think we can look at this hopefully, Mrs. Moreno. It's just one corner of his personality that's causing problems and needs to be worked through."

Looking back, Dr. Pollard, how big a corner would you say it was? Forty-five degrees? Ninety? Would you believe 180? Or did it merely have to be sanded a little?

> Every valley shall be exalted
> And every mountain and hill made low
> The crooked straight
> And the rough places plain . . .

I hummed it as I hurried home and repeated the conversation to Ted. He seemed both irritated that I had called Dr. Pollard without asking him first, and relieved that somebody was doing something—relieved, perhaps, that I cared. He made an appointment for the following day. It did not work out. Ted came back from his appointment to report that although Dr. Pollard agreed he needed intensive treatment, the doctor's own schedule was filled. Therefore he was referring Ted to another psychiatrist in the same building, a Dr. Gray, and the very name seemed reason enough to dread the referral.

Now the suspicions grew rapidly. Everybody was washing their hands of him. Dr. Pollard, an old University graduate himself, had obviously been warned to keep away. And Ted returned from his first appointment with Dr. Gray to report that he was a grim, sinister-looking man who was being paid to exterminate him in a socially acceptable way. He refused to go back. He said we were all in on the plot—whether we wanted to be or not—because we feared for our lives. Ted did not hate me for it, however, he said. On the contrary, he felt sorry for me—sorry for all the trouble. . . .

The fears intensified daily. Ted began staying awake all night. I would often waken at three in the morning to find him crouching by my side of the bed, his face within inches of mine, tears in his eyes, whispering over and over again, "I'm sorry, I'm sorry," like a small frightened child attempting to waken a parent. Sleep became difficult for us both, and I began my new job teaching school more asleep than awake. I adopted a routine of scrounging the kitchen for nutpicks, butcher knives, and hammers each night, making sure they were well hidden before I went to bed. I did not really fear for my life just yet—it was merely a precaution.

And still no one but Ted's parents knew of the change in him. My own relatives did not even know I had been to Albuquerque. There seemed no definite thing to tell anyone. The new quarter began at the University, but Ted, of course, did not go back. He spent his days sitting around the apartment, watching and listening. We were in limbo, waiting for things to get worse.

> Should I, after tea and cakes and ices,
> Have the strength to force the moment to its crisis?

T. S. Eliot's poem became a preoccupation of Ted's. He repeated bits and pieces endlessly.

One evening in February the fears began to mount with unusual intensity. Ted became very agitated and spoke urgently of needing protection. His voice was tense, he perspired with anxiety, and his voice trembled. He decided that a veteran's hospital would be the best place to hide out after all, since the government could be counted on to keep the Communists out. Failing that, he would enter the priesthood and retire to a monastery surrounded by high walls. Who would ever think of finding him there?

No one, I'll admit. I mean, here was this man with an IQ of 184 who always considered himself a freethinker. He had scoffed at his father's sympathies for Joe McCarthy, identified with the rights of the laboring man, and denounced the Pope. From the time his mother had first begun to insist that her bowel movements were beautiful, to her pronouncements that God had given her a mysterious power to heal, he had ridiculed her sainthood, either subtly or openly. And now my mentor, my searcher for the truth, the Great Iconoclast himself, wanted to hide behind a monk's robes for the rest of his natural life. A perfect disguise.

But Ted was serious. There wasn't a moment to lose, he insisted, as he threw a few items in his overnight bag and headed for the car. All the way to the hospital he talked about how he could no longer go without protection. It was time somebody did something, someone took a stand against his enemies. Obviously he couldn't count on me.

The veteran's hospital seemed the logical choice from Ted's point of view because it was government-operated and from mine because it was free. Since Ted had left the insurance company, he had no hospitalization plan.

By the time we reached the admission desk, however, at ten o'clock at night, and sat in the waiting room for a half hour while they located the psychiatrist on call, Ted had calmed down considerably. By the time his name was called and he was ushered into the little white cubicle, he was all smiles, genial and pleasant, secure in the sights and sounds of efficient government people bustling about him. He displayed no aberrant behavior, no particular anxieties, but merely stated that he felt he needed treatment, and no, it was not a service-connected disability. He was promptly refused.

Out in the car again, Ted's fears returned tenfold. He had firmly expected the government to take him, to enfold him in its everlasting arms. If the government wouldn't help him fight the Communists, who would? For another hour he drove aimlessly around the snowy streets, refusing to go home, mumbling to himself, moaning, inconsolable, and finally pulled up to a home for Franciscan monks about midnight. All the lights were out. I tried to talk him into going home and coming back again in the morning, but he was too frightened and I was too tired. So I sank down in the seat while he beat on the door, like the Biblical men of Israel, fleeing to Joshua's cities of refuge.

After some time, a disheveled monk opened the door and asked what Ted wanted. Ted said he wanted to become a Catholic, a brother. He wanted to renounce his life, to live in purity and goodness and Hail Marys to the end of his days.

"And who is that in the car?" asked the monk.

"My wife."

Monks, of course, are used to seeing strange things in the

middle of the night, and we were merely one more, so he invited Ted in for a conference and I promptly fell asleep. I was becoming adept at falling asleep whenever Ted was someone else's responsibility for a while. After forty minutes, the monk came out to the car to tell me what I already knew: my husband was mentally ill and I should have him hospitalized immediately.

There are several misconceptions about the insane. It is presumed, first of all, that a wife, because she is legally bound to her husband, has the power to cart him bodily off where he may have no intention of going. I had not just been Ted's wife for five years, I had been his mattress. And suddenly he had collapsed and I was expected not only to rise up and walk, but to carry him around with me.

The second misconception is that public hospitals will quickly admit patients who are mentally ill. They will not. If a patient is sitting on a tower in Texas picking off people with a rifle, he is deemed sufficiently sick to warrant a bed and immediate treatment. But there are others just as miserable who do not get in so easily.

A third misconception is that psychotic patients are so obviously disoriented and bizarre that they are instantly distinguishable from the general population. It would have been infinitely easier if Ted had been hearing voices or chewing on furniture. It would have been far more convincing if he had been loud or violent, or had exposed himself in front of the courthouse. Instead, he could become quite civilized and disarming, so that, to different people in different situations, he might seem either merely anxious or trembling on the brink of disaster.

After rousing me from sleep and informing me that my husband was crazy (why else would we be parked in front of a monastery at midnight?), the kind priest went back inside to escort Ted to the car and patted his shoulder. He said he was glad of his interest in Catholicism, but felt that Ted needed psychiatric help at the present even more than he needed conversion. And finally, because Ted was exhausted too, we drove back home and managed a few hours' sleep.

We were getting nowhere. Ted would sleep fitfully during the day while I was teaching, then prowl the apartment at night. He would sit tensely at the window, watching for shadows on the street below, or else crouch beside the bed, watching me sleep. I became alarmed each time I woke and found him out of bed. I was unable to sleep unless I knew just where he was and what he was doing. In the evenings, I found myself on edge if he passed behind my chair, and each afternoon, when I turned the key in the lock, I braced myself for disaster.

And yet, we continued to make love, and each time I wanted to weep for him. I encircled him in my arms, as though the warmth and security might somehow work their magic and make him well. They made him sleep, for a few hours at least, but did not make him well.

And then one afternoon I arrived home to find Ted gone. I checked the bathroom, the closet. Nothing was missing. His clothes were all in order. I checked the fire escape, then the basement, and finally the park behind the building. The car was gone also.

I went back upstairs and prepared dinner, waiting with increased alarm. Six o'clock came, then seven. I heard his footsteps on the stairs and, as the door opened, I noticed that he came inside rather stiffly, a strange expression on his face, and went immediately into the closet. I heard the rustling of paper and the thunk of something hitting the floor.

"What is it, Ted?" I asked, when he came back out.

He gave no answer, but took up the usual watch by the

window. I went in the closet and Ted made no move to stop me. There lay a long package marked Sears. I opened one end and found myself staring into the barrel of a rifle.

Perhaps it was what we both had been waiting for—something that would force a decision and make it easy.

"What are you going to do with this, Ted?"

For once he was definite.

"Tonight's it," he said, and I noticed that his voice shook, his words came rapidly. "This is the night they're coming to get me. I know. I heard. And I'm going to be ready."

I thought of the woman who lived across the hall, who usually got home about nine. Would he misjudge her footsteps and fire through the door? If a Fuller Brush man or an Avon lady rapped at our apartment, would he gun them down? Or would he sit at the window after I went to sleep and aim at the shadows on the sidewalk?

I put on my coat, ran all the way to the drugstore, and called Dr. Pollard at home.

"Call the police," he said helpfully.

I told him that I couldn't. I felt that that would be the end of Ted's trust in me. I could imagine the scene it would create . . . the terror in Ted as the police cars closed in around the building. I couldn't do it.

"What do you want me to do then?" the doctor asked.

"I want to bring Ted to your house so you can talk him out of the gun. He won't go back to Dr. Gray. You're the only one he will listen to."

Miraculously, Dr. Pollard agreed to do it, and I was grateful.

As I started back up the stairs to our third-floor apartment, I realized that my own life could be in danger. Ted would certainly know I had gone to call someone, as we had no phone in the apartment, by his own preference. He would

70

undoubtedly expect the worst. Perhaps he had really bought the gun to use on me, and this would be his excuse. Then again, I knew that I was the only person Ted had left. He had alienated everyone else. I tried to make my footsteps sound familiar, so he would know it was me, but who knows his own footsteps that intimately?

I had left the door open, and called his name before I went inside, my heart pounding. I half expected to see him lying on the floor in a pool of blood. Instead, he was sitting by the window, calmly loading the rifle, and examining a bullet carefully.

I could hardly believe what happened next. He ate the bullet. He obviously suspected that the clerk had sold him blanks instead of bullets and so he bit one open to make sure. And then it disappeared.

I told Ted that Dr. Pollard wanted to see him immediately at his home, and he offered no resistance. I expected that he would bring the gun along, possibly rammed down one trouser leg, but he did not. So I went downstairs beside that living powder keg and we drove to the doctor's house near the University. I was bringing Ted ostensibly to be talked out of his gun, and he'd left it behind. What did I do now?

Perhaps it was my own imagination, but the porch and steps of the doctor's home looked as though the Pollard children had been whisked from their play and secluded in a room upstairs. A sled was lying on the steps and a mitten near the front door. In the entrance hall lay a half-eaten cracker that had been dropped in the haste of the mass exodus. Here we come, everybody, the crack shot of East Lake Boulevard. If he doesn't gun you down, he'll burp and blow us all to Kingdom Come.

Dr. Pollard met us at the door with a firm handshake and a warm smile. Ted responded enthusiastically. Homecoming week. The Famous Alumni Handshake.

"Glad to see you," lied the doctor.

"You're looking good," Ted said.

It is a marvelous feeling to find yourself in the presence of wisdom, even when that wisdom makes a mistake. I have always remembered Dr. Pollard fondly, for his was a voice of reason in the first several years of our marriage, and on the few occasions when I went to see him myself, before he recommended a therapist for me, he was kind, reassuring, and dared to suggest that what Ted thought about me in terms of inferiority and lack of intelligence or sophistication might possibly tell more about Ted than it did about me. Now, as his warm smile enveloped us both, I felt a flood of relief. Ted was his problem, not mine.

"Well!" said the doctor, sitting down across from us in his black leather chair, and I realized what a chance he must have felt he was taking. I had neglected to tell him that the gun was a rifle a yard long, and perhaps he thought it was concealed in Ted's pocket. Did he himself have a pistol handy, I wondered? Were there security men watching from behind the folding screen, ready to fire if Ted so much as scratched his crotch? Was there a paddy wagon waiting at the back entrance, perhaps? Three taps on the floor, and would Mrs. Pollard, sitting upstairs, sound the alarm?

I worshiped the doctor for allowing us to come. I wished I could turn and walk back out and leave Ted sitting forever face-to-face with Freud's disciple. Somehow, I thought, just getting him here was 90 percent of the problem. Now the good doctor would work his magic, clear up Ted's confusion, and tell us what to do next.

There is no such magic, I was to find out again and again in the course of the next three years. But there was honesty. Dr. Pollard talked calmly and directly to Ted. He pointed out that Ted was indeed sick, and that in this condition he was not in a position to make intelligent decisions for himself. The best thing Ted could do would be to trust those of us who were closest to him and rely on our judgment as to what should be done. He suggested that Ted give up all ideas of trying to work this through by himself, that this could only lead to desperate situations, and that he should voluntarily hospitalize himself at once so as to avoid having to be committed.

The panic bubbled up in me again. It was becoming an old refrain. I explained how we had already gone this route, but because Ted would undoubtedly be calm when he got to the hospital, he would again be refused.

It was also a professional dilemma, I realized, because Ted was officially Dr. Gray's patient now, and Dr. Pollard could not ethically refer him himself. He suggested, instead, that I simply tell the doctors at the hospital that Dr. Pollard had recommended immediate admission, we shook hands all around, and off we went again into the night.

The road to anywhere was never direct. First Ted had to drive around for several hours going over all the pros and cons, and by the time I convinced him that there was to be no pulling back this time, it was almost eleven. Life would have been far simpler if I had known how to drive.

The consultation was long and "iffy." Three psychiatrists examined Ted, one interviewed me, and finally the doctor on call said that she had been to school with Dr. Pollard and respected his judgment, so Ted was taken to a ward and I was left to fill out the papers.

It was twelve-thirty when I had finished. I realized that Ted's car would stay here in the parking lot indefinitely and that I would have to get home some other way. The receptionist called a cab. Halfway home, I discovered that the meter already registered more than I had in my purse. There was only enough money at home to get me to work the next day and back. Ted had the rest with him. And so the cab driver took me to a bus stop at one o'clock in the morning, let me out in ankle-deep snow, and it was three-thirty when I finally made the last bus transfer and reached our apartment, half frozen and exhausted beyond belief.

I slept as though I were embalmed. I slept as though I had been drugged, doped, and was drunk out of my mind. The alarm had been set for six, but only the constant ringing of the phone at ten o'clock woke me up.

It was the school secretary. She asked if I planned to come in, and I stared aghast at the clock. I told her that my husband had been sick all night, and I was afraid I would not make it. She reminded me that I was a professional person and was expected to be responsible enough to call in—that my twenty-nine pupils were roaming the halls and creating a disturbance, and she hoped it would not happen again.

I knew it could remain a secret no longer. The following day I faced the others in the teachers' lounge before classes.

"Heard your husband was sick," someone said. "Nothing serious, I hope."

"I'm afraid it is," I said. "Ted had a nervous breakdown and was hospitalized."

With those few words, the hardest thing in the world became the easiest. The hiding and excusing and protecting and shielding and lying of the past six months had been infinitely more difficult than letting it all come out. I found instant empathy, support, and simple human kindness.

"And I thought I had problems," one woman said, and they drew the wagons around me.

The first thing facing me was the income tax. Not only had I never heard of Form 1040 in my life, but I had never balanced a checkbook or paid the rent. Suddenly all sorts of things were arriving in the mail to make me feel inade-

quate—car insurance, life insurance policies, registration re-
newal forms, and bank statements.

The second thing I faced was to tell my own parents about
Ted.

There is something about telling friends and coworkers
that is different from telling bad news to one's family. Although friends are sorry for you and wish you well and ask
to help, they are—for the most part—able to turn you off and
on at will. They don't feel responsible for you. They are sad
whenever they think about you and the trouble you are going
through, but they don't think about you all the time.

Families, though, are something else. There is a communal
nerve in families connecting one member to another, and
when one is hurt, they all suffer. However much I wanted to
save my parents from this latest news, I knew I could not
hide it any longer in my letters. So I told them, as I'd told my
friends at work, that Ted had suffered a nervous breakdown.

"Nervous breakdown" is a polite phrase, I've discovered,
for all sorts of things one cannot explain. It was a term I used
to minimize a frankly psychotic condition. It is what some
parents use to describe a son who drops out of college and
wants to bum around. It is what wives use to denote husbands
who are suddenly unfaithful. It is the Great American
Catchall to explain any condition which displeases us, and
suddenly all sorts of people were confessing that they knew
what I was going through because they or their spouses had
had a nervous breakdown only last year. But none of them,
it turned out upon questioning, sat at a window with a loaded
rifle waiting for Communists to crawl up the side of the
building.

My parents, however, did not find comfort in any memories
they may have had of friends who had been to the brink and
back again. There was nothing at all they could do either for

75

Ted or for me, and that made it even worse for them. My father, I discovered to my surprise years later, went to visit Ted frequently, when he had health problems of his own I did not even know about. My mother prayed and wrote encouraging letters. What more could one ask? This ordinary family of forty-four sane and sensible relatives had never faced a situation like this before. We wrote each other optimistic notes about how fortunate Ted was to live so close to a veteran's hospital where the treatment was free. We reminded each other of Ted's great intelligence and fine education, as though these would win him Brownie points on the ward and preferential treatment from the doctors. He would be rescued from his madness, in other words, because he was so eminently worth saving. We attributed the whole thing to overwork at the University, and said how the coming spring and summer, away from his books, would certainly bring about improvement.

I began telling the truth to friends who called, to neighbors I met at the co-op on Saturdays. I found myself being invited over for dinner, out to movies, called on the phone (which I had installed), encouraged, supported.

"Thank you for sharing this with me," one man said when I blurted out what had happened, and I thought this was a lovely thing to have said.

Two of our friends were a couple we had known for some time. He was a musician, an accomplished pianist, and she was an artist of oriental descent. They had approached city hall three times with witnesses in tow, and each time had managed to get into an argument and call off the wedding ceremony before it happened. When they did finally manage to go through with it, each was so furious at the other that they spent the first week of their honeymoon in separate apartments. Dale was sullen, moody—he even *looked* like Beethoven—and Anna was fairly bursting with life, forever talking in a rapid-fire delivery, direct and disarming. They were among the first I called about Ted, and Anna responded instantly by coming over to spend the night.

I needed comfort, but I didn't, I discovered, need Anna. After an inconsequential evening of supper and talk and music, we went to sleep on the sofa bed, and I wakened at two to find her curled closely behind me, one hand caressing my belly and moving on down between my legs. I rolled over on my back and lay staring up at the ceiling, eyes wide. The madman had been replaced already by problem number two. Anna lay on her side of the bed, waiting, but I did not respond, and in the morning we parted as amicably and innocently as if it had been a mutual dream, nothing more.

The fact was, I was surviving quite well. I was surprised to discover I could survive at all. By following the tax forms from the previous year, I managed to complete 1040 without help. I got new license plates for the Studebaker, paid the rent, and balanced the checkbook—enormously proud of these small accomplishments which other wives had been doing for years. I even took the rifle back to Sears.

"Yes, Ma'am, what can we do for you?"

"I'd like to return this rifle, please. The receipt's on the package."

The salesman frowned and unwrapped the gun. "Did you want to exchange it for something else?"

"No, I want a refund."

"Something wrong with the gun?"

"No, we just decided we didn't really need it."

"Didn't get any big game with it, huh? Ha ha."

The man irritated me with his casualness, his flip. I wondered if perhaps he was the man who had sold it to Ted.

"My husband was mentally ill when he purchased it," I said coldly, "and I was afraid he might kill someone."

There are certain little phrases which are extremely powerful, I discovered. That Sears had made the mistake of selling a rifle to a deranged man showed in every line of the man's face and he was flip no longer. He assured me there would be no trouble getting the refund. He seemed weak with relief to have the gun in his hands again. He rushed about getting the credit slips in order, and I was glad he accepted the box of bullets without counting them. I was afraid there would have to be explanations.

("There's one bullet missing, Ma'am."

"Yes, I know. I'm afraid it's in my husband."

"Oh, no! You don't mean . . . ?"

"Yes. He ate it.")

I was given Thursday afternoons off, with pay, to visit Ted. Periodically I was allowed to talk with the doctor as well as a psychiatric social worker assigned to the case. I soon discovered that what the hospital expected of me as a wife was as unrealistic as what I had expected of it as a medical facility.

What I had expected of the hospital was that it would turn my husband back into the man he used to be, if not better. That through slow, careful, psychiatric counseling, Ted could face his fear of the University (mother?) and the business world (father?) and find out where his real interests lay so that he could become his own man, independent of both, frightened of neither, and hence be able to relate to them in a kind, yet strong, way. Nothing major, you understand. Just a quick little overhaul.

What the hospital expected of me was to distort reality just enough so that Ted and I could exist somewhere off the hospital grounds and thus free another bed for someone who might need it more.

My first encounter with the social worker came the day after I had completed the income tax form. She asked how

78

I was managing at home, and I told her much better than I'd expected. She looked sad.

"One of the problems our men have," she said, using the editorial "our" as though her own husband were on the ward, "is a feeling of uselessness, and it's best if we don't let them know just how well we are coping without them."

I stared. Did she know what she was saying? Did she realize it had taken all these years for me to function without a male continually at my side, and now that I had timidly poked my head out of the sand, she wanted me to retreat again? If I were in the hospital, would it have helped to think that Ted was a perfect idiot when it came to household things, and that the apartment was collapsing around him? Wouldn't the simple knowledge that one was missed, was needed as a person, companion, and lover, be the crucial factor in feeling wanted?

"But I *am* managing well!" I protested. "I never thought I could do it! I'm sure that Ted has been worrying about the income tax, but I did it myself!"

"I know," she said sweetly, "but we don't have to tell him that, do we?"

("What are we going to do about the income tax, Phyllis?"

"Well, it's really strange, but when I woke up this morning, I discovered it had mailed itself off."

"You mean you actually got it done?"

"Well . . . I . . . uh . . . no, you see, I got the janitor to come up and help me out, and he said to tell you we've got a refund of fifty-five dollars coming.")

The veteran's hospital was a huge cluster of red brick buildings, some connected by brick tunnels, in a campus atmosphere. Each building had a number, and one could tell the psychiatric facilities from the others by the heavy metal screens over the windows.

79

I arrived at this massive government hospital on a bus along with a crowd of other visiting relatives, each carrying a present of candy or paperbacks or magazines. It was easy to determine which were relatives of patients in for nothing more than an appendectomy or hernia, for they laughed and joked with each other, and the weekly jaunt was simply a holiday excursion.

As we all surged up the main drive, little groups broke off here and there heading for different buildings until finally a little cluster of us were left, destined for Building 51. We were the untalkative bunch. We looked at each other furtively to see what kind of personality traits had sent other relatives on a race from reality, and were grateful when we found a flaw that we didn't possess. ("See how rigidly he walks; anybody who walks like that would drive his son crazy, all right.") ("Notice the nervous way she keeps picking at her dress. Anyone who lived with her would be bound to be nutty.") It is impossible to look at relatives of psychiatric patients as separate entities. We were all tied somehow to the deranged member of our families by an invisible umbilical cord, and the unspoken fear remained in each of us that we carried seeds of that madness, either to awaken at a later time in ourselves, or to push still another relative over the brink.

We did not see the wards. We gave our names at the desk, along with the name of the person we wished to visit. Then we all sat down in a large bile-green reception room with a row of hard chairs lining the wall, and waited till the patients were brought down in their ghastly wrinkled army pajamas with legs that were always too long or too short.

The sicker ones did not come, only those who were ambulatory and in reasonable control of themselves. They came skulking, unsmiling, hands hanging loosely at their sides, eyes averted, like prisoners of war. Once in the room, the relatives greeted them in maddeningly cheerful voices, telling them again and again how marvelous they looked. Lies. All lies.

Ted was not improving. He was morose, sullen, apathetic. He was not sleeping well, not eating. He saw no point to life, to living, to planning for anything except his death, and that, he told me, had already been planned by "the others." After a few weeks, the doctor decided on shock treatments, and Ted was terrified at the thought.

"They'll pull you out of your depression so that the doctor can reach you through therapy," I soothed, and when I visited him after the first treatment, I was convinced it had been the right thing to do.

Ted was a new man. He seemed very much like the Ted I had known at his best, as though he were awakening from a long sleep. He was confused. What was he doing in this place? He wanted to go home, to make love, to listen to records. He was affectionate, passionate. There was so much to do, to talk about. Why should he stay here?

I greeted him as though he had been away for a year. I kissed him, caressed him, and cared not at all about the frowns of patients and relatives across the room who felt that such happiness was out of place.

"Welcome back," I whispered in his ear.

But he had questions. What had happened to bring him here? He just couldn't remember. . . .

I told him. I told him about the gun and the midnight trip to the monastery. I told him about the Communists and the sleeplessness and the trip to Albuquerque and Dr. Gerber and all the rest. He shook his head. He couldn't understand. All he wanted was to go home. We loved some more, and could have been on stage at Constitution Hall for all it mattered. Our good-bye was a lingering kiss, long and tender. . . .

I had an appointment to see his doctor the following week before I saw Ted. I entered his office full of praise for him, for the hospital, for shock treatments, for Freud, Jung, and Adler, Inc.

The doctor did not seem to share my enthusiasm.

"How do you feel that your husband is progressing?" he asked.

I burbled on about what a fine job they were doing. I told him about my last visit and how affectionate Ted had been and how he had forgotten everything and I had to tell him what had happened.

The doctor was noticeably upset.

"Tell him *nothing*," he scolded, as though I should have known better, "except that he has been sick. Especially don't remind him of any of those fears. Shock treatments make him forget. We don't *want* him to remember."

Slowly the realization came that we would never be able to talk frankly with each other again, Ted and I. There would always be something between us, always something I knew that he didn't, always a secret, an unspeakable thing.

("But what was *wrong* with me, Phyllis? What were the symptoms?"

"You were just very sick, dear."

"You mean I was throwing up? Peeing all over the place?"

"It's better not to talk about it."

"You mean it was worse than that? Was I attacking people? Going around naked?"

"Ted, it's really better if you don't know."

"My god, what was I doing? I'll go mad if you don't tell me!")

When I saw Ted a half hour later, I scarcely recognized

82

him. He was gaunt, bitter, sarcastic, scornful. They were killing him, he said—torturing him. There was a terrible pain in his chest since the latest shock treatment. It hurt like hell to breathe. Why had I brought him here to die? Why didn't they just shoot him and get it over with? What had he ever done to deserve this? Had I no pity, no mercy?

The next few visits were the same. Ted sat drowsily, eyes closing, as though drugged, sometimes half asleep. He could not remember things that had happened the day before and it bothered him. He felt that they were tampering with his mind, his intelligence. They were fixing him so he could never get a Ph.D. even if he wanted one. They were turning him into someone else. They were using his body to house someone else's brain. Soon he wouldn't know me at all. He wouldn't even exist. And the pain in his chest continued. It hurt with every breath he took, but no one would believe him.

When I came again, Ted was like a small, frightened child. He greeted me wistfully, hopefully, pleading, almost, with the news that he had been taken to X-ray for the pain and it was discovered that he had cracked a rib during one of the shock treatments. Now wouldn't I take him home? Please, hadn't he suffered enough? Wouldn't I reconsider, and let him live?

FOUR

UNKNOWN TO ME then, we were to become nomads, Ted and I. Like the Israelites on their way to Canaan, we would search for the Promised Land.

Ted's overriding wish was to get out of the hospital and leave the Big City, to start a new life somewhere else. As the months passed and winter melted away into spring, the doctor allowed him an occasional visit home on weekends to see how well he adjusted to life on the outside.

The visits were very sweet to him. There were his favorite dishes for supper, his records, his books, privacy, and sex. There were soft Sunday mornings to lie in bed with our arms around each other, the newspaper outside the door, and hot rolls with our coffee. He even enjoyed the freedom of the bus ride to and from the hospital, the mixing with normal people, all intensifying his desire to be out. And because he did not try to shoot the janitor or run away or walk around the block naked, the administration set his discharge for June.

Our plan was to take a vacation tour through Wisconsin to find the "ideal" community, our blue heaven, and settle down for the rest of our natural lives with No-Great-Dreams-Whatsoever. It made sense to me. It made sense to his doctors. Even Dr. Pollard, when told of the idea over the phone, said it might be a fine idea. The one person who didn't think much of it was the school superintendent who had hired me. What made me so sure that Ted could escape his problems by moving away? And what about my own life? I had a real future as a teacher, he said, and they had scheduled me for a second grade class in the fall. What about my own identity, my own dreams?

Identity? Dreams? I heard, but I didn't understand. I was Ted's wife forever after. I had promised it in front of the entire congregation. I had promised Ted in the dozens of letters I wrote him at the University to make him the happiest man alive once we were married, and obviously he was one of the most miserable. The future was all cut out for me. The work ahead was enormous. The Ruth Complex— whither thou goest I will go. And so we miraculously got the Studebaker started after it had been on the parking lot for six months, packed it with suitcases, and set off for Wisconsin to choose a new home town.

The thing about optimism is that when you batter it down one place, it springs up another. As we looked over one city after another—Madison, Fond du Lac, Green Bay, Appleton, Oshkosh, Neenah, Stevens Point, Eau Claire, La Crosse—I approached each one as though it were our future home. I smiled at the residents in each business district as Ted made the usual trip to the employment office. I would be the "Carol" of *Main Street,* but far from being disillusioned by the narrow-mindedness of a small town, I would

85

welcome the solitude. I would write away the hours while Ted regenerated himself, and would come to know the townspeople as good-hearted souls, filled with the steady virtues of loyalty and kindness. Here I would find a respite from the evils of the Big City which had shaken us down to the starting line again.

But it soon became obvious that Wisconsin was not our Canaan. No matter how lovely the city, the milk and honey turned bitter as Ted discovered first one flaw and then another in each one. I finally ceased thinking, "Here's where we'll shop," and "Here's where we'll ride our bikes," in each new place we stopped. The three weeks we had allowed for the trip were almost over, and so we crossed into Minnesota, chose a city there, and rented a third-floor apartment out of desperation. Then we went back home to pack. Like the Israelites on their flight from Egypt, we worked rapidly, as though any minute Pharaoh might change his mind. And finally, putting the plagues behind us, we said good-bye to East Lake Boulevard and headed for our new home.

The big difference I noticed now in Ted was his driving. From a rigid, cautious, conservative driver who was religious about rules, Ted now drove much too fast. His attention wandered, his eyes left the road, and he sometimes rounded a corner so carelessly that the wheels went over the curb. When I cautioned him to pay more attention, he did not seem to know what I was talking about.

By midsummer we were Minnesotans. Ted passed the Civil Service exam and was hired by the post office as a mail sorter. I located the library and the shops, and decided—in what must have been the maddest moment of my entire life—to show my faith in Ted and in our future by having a baby. We would be a family. Here in our Minnesota hideaway, Ted would be free of academic pressure and would find the love and security that would ultimately make him whole. So I bid farewell to my diaphragm, announced my decision to Ted, and waited to be fertilized.

Ted's job was difficult. He was required to memorize every street, with its range of house numbers, in the entire city, and his ability to do so had been affected by the shock treatments. Day after day we spent our afternoons memorizing, quizzing, memorizing some more. He found it tedious and boring. The job itself was monotonous, lonely, and not unlike a prison. All the sorters, Ted explained, stood at their stations in one great room, while high above, behind one-way glass, the supervisors watched the inmates to be sure they did not take the millions of quarters and box tops destined for General Mills.

As the weeks went on, Ted put in applications for other government positions more in line with his capabilities—mathematician, cartographer, English instructor. . . . But each time the requests for interviews came through—and they came because his background *was* impressive—there was a flaw somewhere in the offer that only Ted could see—a clause, a condition—something that caught his eye and made him wary. And so he turned them all down.

Slowly the security of having been lodged in a government hospital and being hired as a government employee began to wear thin, as Ted went through his ritual of filling out forms for jobs he would never take. The ploy of running away to be protected by Uncle Sam began to show through. But I ignored it all. The way we minimize our lovers' faults during courtship is nothing compared to the way we convince ourselves that serious problems in a spouse are perhaps nothing more than minor aberrations.

Ted was placed on the four-to-midnight shift. We found ourselves eating breakfast at eleven, lunch at three, and dinner at one in the morning. It was difficult to adjust. The noises which had been evening sounds back home—laughter

87

and music from neighboring apartments—now woke us in the mornings long before we were ready to get up. The doorbell and phone were a constant annoyance. In the evenings, when I was ready to socialize, other people went to bed. So I wrote—the salvation of the cloistered.

Whom did I write for? Would you believe magazines called *Woodmen of the World, Gospel Trumpet,* or *Hand in Hand? Covenant Trails, Free-to-Be,* or the *New York Mirror? Teaching Tools, The Instructor,* and *Elementary English?* I was no Eudora Welty taking sixteen years to write *Losing Battles* or Katherine Anne Porter taking twenty to write *Ship of Fools.* I was turning out stories like biscuits on a floured board, and about all one could say for them was that they sold.

It began to irritate Ted that the mail was mostly for me, that the checks, however small, kept coming. It was he, after all, who had traveled, he who had majored in English, and he—obviously—who should be published, if either of us was.

"You'll make it," he said to me sarcastically one evening. *"They'll* see to that."

It was as though a door had opened and a cold wind were sweeping through, stopping the clocks and freezing us into statues which stared at each other across the living room. Had I heard right? They? The faceless, nameless "they" again, who inhabited walls, cupboards, and ceiling fixtures? The "they" we had scrupulously not discussed since Ted's discharge, who had driven us out of one state and into another? Yes, "they" were coming again with their chariots and swords, and there was no Dr. Pollard this time to offer us refuge.

I wanted to scream that I would not stand for this kind of talk any longer. I wanted to prohibit these fears from our lives, to forbid Ted ever to speak of them again. If he could not control the monsters which crept unbidden into his mind, I wanted him to put on at least a semblance of the well-adjusted male going confidently off to work each day. But even to me, the image was ludicrous. The demons were multiplying like a fertilized cell.

Suddenly Ted wanted to join a church for protection. He wanted to call Dr. Pollard long distance. He wanted to send for his father, write his mother, move to Patuxent Naval Base, and then he wanted none of it. Frantically I retrieved my diaphragm, but it was too late. Ten days later I discovered that I was pregnant.

The Red Sea began to close over me. I felt that Ted and I were locked together in a fatal embrace. I was sickened with my own stupidity and could scarcely believe I'd been so naïve.

I had often fantasied the moment I would tell Ted that I expected his child. Those six children we'd talked about in our courtship letters were supposed to bring us profound joy and fulfillment. I had always imagined that Ted would take me in his arms in a gesture of love and gratitude, and the fact that I was becoming a mother as well as a wife would make him cherish me forever.

Ted took the news impassively as he stared out the window at two men passing below—agents, no doubt. He made no response. He said absolutely nothing. The child-to-be was only one more person against him.

"Doesn't it mean anything to you at all?" I cried, anger and fright welling up in me simultaneously. "I'm going to have a baby, Ted! You've got to take care of us! You've got to be responsible!"

His eyes never left the window. "I can't take care of anybody if I'm dead," he replied. "My first responsibility is to stay alive."

I did not know, in the days that followed, if I was ill or

simply sick with fright. I seemed to have a fever. I trembled continuously and was seized with chills. I wrapped myself in blankets and sat in a chair in the kitchen, moving only when I had to. Ted came and went, ignoring me.

Pregnancy, no matter how much I wanted children, was something I had always feared. I feared the nausea, the swelling of veins in the legs, the stretched abdomen, and the strain on the body organs. I expected childbirth to be something akin to an auto accident, with ripping flesh and blood galore. If my defloration was painful, think what childbirth must be!

When I was only four, I was taken to a funeral parlor to see a beloved aunt who had died in childbirth, the dead infant in her arms. When I was ten, I read an article on pain in a magazine, and—in an accompanying chart—various pains were listed in order of severity. The mildest, according to the chart, was a cigarette burn. The most intense was childbirth. Childbirth, then, was obviously like being burned by thousands of cigarettes simultaneously. I never forgave the editor for that misinformation.

Yet I always wanted to be a mother, despite the risks and the pain. Other women had had babies and went on to have more. With a loving, supportive husband by my side, I could do it too. And now I was alone and the thing was growing inside me, a creature I did not even know, a babe that would be as welcome in our household as a staph infection in a surgical ward. My body would be distended and over-whelmed and ugly, and the rift between Ted and me would be all the greater. When I needed encouragement the most, Ted would have none to give. I would have two children to care for nine months hence. And the thought that perhaps in this small fetus, the seeds of schizophrenia might already be growing made me weak, sending off waves of panic.

Madness was multiplying all around and in me, and there was no escape.

Ted suddenly wanted to join a Lutheran church, and went to see the pastor of a nearby parish. Within minutes after the conference was over, I got a call at home.

"Your husband has just left my office," the pastor said. "I wonder if you realize that he's a very sick man."

Do something, the pastor's tone seemed to imply. But could anyone please tell me what? Ted trusted no one, especially doctors. He did not even trust me. He credited me with "wanting" to help him, but insisted that eventually "they" would make me do as they said.

It is the life force, I suppose, or possibly only habit, that keeps us doing our daily mundane tasks in the knowledge that crisis is most probably around the corner. In fact, it was habit and the repetition of mundane tasks which offered the only security I knew. I grew fond of making the bed because it was predictably rumpled every morning. I awaited the arrival of the daily paper and the postman because I knew they would arrive as scheduled. The ritual of taking trash to the incinerator and picking up shirts at the laundry brought a kind of peace that few could appreciate because it meant that I was still alive, still functioning like everyone else, in spite of something happening to my body that I did not want, and a life I could not control.

Ted went to work every day and I continued to submit material to editors as though we were any normal married couple going about our separate tasks. I knew, however, that I needed other people, or would soon need them, more desperately than ever, and leaped at the chance to join a young couples' group at the Lutheran church. We were going back in time, back to the meat loaf discussions and parlor games, but I didn't care. I was desperate for friends.

91

There was to be a September picnic, and for an entire week Ted was obsessed with the invitation. Who had called us? Was it, perhaps, a Russian sounding name? No? Then it was probably an English name used as a front. Was it a man or woman? Did I detect an accent? Why on earth had I said we would go? Didn't I realize it was only an excuse to get him out in the country where he could be more easily abducted?

When Saturday came, windy and rainy, the picnic was canceled. I expected Ted to feel relieved, perhaps even a little silly. But insanity has a way of becoming more so. Ted stood calmly at the window, watching it pour, and announced that the Communists had perfected ways of changing the weather at will, and had undoubtedly decided to kill him some other way, another time. Hence, the rain.

It was too much. I became a shrew—a shrieking, pregnant shrew, blind with exasperation. What did it take to reach this man—this person of superior intelligence who argued like a kindergarten child? Was it possible he believed this nonsense, or was it a slow deliberate attempt to drive me mad along with him?

There can be nothing more infuriating than the paranoid who places himself in the center of the universe and interprets every event, no matter how small or how large, as having the greatest significance for him. At the base of the paranoia is a supremely exaggerated delusion of self-importance, and it is no joke that such patients play the role of Napoleon or Jesus Christ.

Because he was not babbling gibberish, because he could feed and clothe himself and drive to work each day, because he had once been known for his intellectual prowess and his ability to debate in a rational manner, I made, many times over, the mistake that most families of paranoids make —the attempt to reason, appealing to logic. In doing so, I experienced again and again the futility one discovers in working with such patients. I well understood the hospital's reluctance to take him in and Dr. Pollard's relief to see him go.

Weekly, daily, sometimes hourly, the following dialogue would take place between us in endless variations:

"What have you ever done, Ted, that would make the Communists want to kill you?"

"They want you, and they have to get rid of me first."

"But *I* don't want *them!* I don't *know* any Communists. I wouldn't recognize a Communist if one appeared in full uniform!"

"But they know you."

"All right. Let's assume it's true. If they really want me, don't you think they would have taken me by now? Why would they have to get rid of you first?"

"Because I know too much. I know the way they operate at the University."

"Then what are they waiting for? Why don't they just knock you off—put a knife in your back or something?"

"That would be too simple. I have to suffer first. The timing has to be right."

"Don't you think you've suffered enough already? Can't you see how you're torturing yourself?"

"Maybe you care, but they don't."

"Do you really think the Russians would have spent the millions of dollars necessary to make it rain last Saturday—assuming that they could—just to keep us from going to a picnic?"

"The Communists can do anything."

"But why couldn't we have gone to the damn picnic anyway, whether they'd changed their minds or not? Why would they have to spend a million dollars making it rain?"

"That's just the way they operate."

"Ted, has it ever occurred to you that you just aren't that important? What egotism! What delusions of grandeur! Can't you see the absurdity in all of this? You're arguing like a child. You've got answers for everything, no matter how ridiculous. If you wanted to leave the University, I wouldn't have cared. You didn't have to invent stories about the Communists chasing you out. Why should the Communists do all this for *you?*"

"Because I know too much."

Ad infinitum. It was as though he felt that he had to be punished for his marvelous intelligence, his knowledge, and the success he might become.

Did he at least smile? Did he seem even a little embarrassed at his inane answers? No, this former member of the high school debate team did not, this paragon of Quantitative Inquiry saw nothing ridiculous in it at all.

Nor did it occur to me to leave him. I still clung to the belief that if I could just get him in treatment somewhere with a skillful psychiatrist, there might be a breakthrough. Leaving him would have been like walking out on a frightened though belligerent child. One simply does not abandon a person who seems so helpless and, in spite of his carping, so dependent. I nourished the fantasy that some day when he was well, the doctors would tell him all that had happened, and he would look at me with grateful, misty eyes and love me forever and ever because of my loyalty. At long last I would have proved myself worthy. Which of us was the sicker? Why did I have to go to such lengths to get the love of a man?

October arrived, and mercifully, a miscarriage. As some women weep with joy at the birth of a child, I wept with the relief of losing one. I sat on the toilet as huge clumps of blood poured out of me, dizzy with gratitude. And yet there was a sadness too that I could not explain. Perhaps, at the loss of the fetus, I was also losing a friend, the one person who could have given my life meaning again and brought back the joy. Now I was alone, and the distance between Ted and me was greater than ever. I told him I had lost the baby. He made no response. The Great Stone Face had been spared paternity after all.

As autumn became winter and Christmas approached, the volume of mail at the post office grew heavier. Ted was under pressure to work faster just when his fears were becoming stronger and more distracting. When his job rating came through, the supervisor graded him "poor."

We talked of Christmas, and there was the unspoken assumption that it would be the last one we would have together. We both felt we were reaching some sort of breaking point, as though we would wait to see who cracked up first. It was a sad time, and my grief and pity for him alternated with feelings of rage for what this was doing to our life, our plans.

Ted saw significance in the most mundane detail. Every movement of his body told him his fortune for the day. Decisions began to overwhelm him. Should he sit in the green chair or the gray one? Gray is the color of death, so he couldn't choose that, but green is the grass that covers the grave. Should he stand, then? Ah, that was it. The Communists had planted the green and gray chairs in our living room (actually, the salesman who sold them to us had been Communist, influencing our choice). They knew he would be unable to sit in either of these chairs on this particular morning, forcing him to stand so that he would be a better target for the sharpshooter on the roof next door. A true Rube Goldberg creation.

Should he wear a jacket or a coat, brown gloves or black?

Should he eat facing the window or the wall, part his hair on the right or left, answer the phone on the third or fourth ring?

> Do I dare
> Disturb the universe?
> In a minute there is time
> For decisions and revisions which a minute will reverse.

Whatever he chose could well decide his fate, and it was imperative to know the hidden meaning behind everything. Consequently, he was paralyzed with ambivalence and began doing nothing at all.

A week before Christmas, Ted gave up his job at the post office by simply not going to work. We did not discuss it, but decided instead to splurge, and bought the most beautiful Christmas tree we could find, rich with the scent of pine. Ted was subdued and sad and agonized. As I put the lights on it, he sat on the couch methodically breaking all ornaments which were duplicates of each other, though he could not explain why.

I called my family one evening to tell them that Ted was ill again and that we would not be coming down for Christmas as we had planned. And then I broke down and cried. It was a relief to let it all out and hear a sympathetic voice respond—to allow my grief to erupt, knowing that someone sane was listening—someone who cared. I began to realize how long it had been since I had experienced a normal response to feelings.

"Phyllis, I'm so sorry," Mother said, and it was the best thing she could have said. No offer to help, because there was nothing she could do. No suggestions because they were futile, no assurance that things would be better, because she knew it would be a lie. Just a sharing of feeling, and that's what I wanted.

Days passed as though they had all happened before, as though we were on a giant revolving wheel, the same scenes destined to play again and again, the revival of hope alternating with a plunge into despair. I made a sudden decision to force Ted to seek help by withdrawing from the hassle altogether. Perhaps the fact that I had tried to comfort him, reason with him, argue with him gave him some sort of satisfaction, and if I could remain totally neutral and detached, he would be shocked into doing something for himself.

One evening, Ted began a tirade against me and my alliance with "men who would destroy him." Somehow I was to blame. It was I who had prevented him from staying in Albuquerque with his parents. I had signed the papers admitting him to the veteran's hospital and therefore I was responsible for his broken rib. I was a witch in disguise.

I said nothing. After a few minutes I stood up and left the room, but Ted followed, his voice getting louder, more agitated. And finally, when I still did not respond, he whirled me around, gripped my face between his hands and held me like a vise, while he repeated his accusations one by one. His hands seemed unusually strong, far stronger than I'd ever realized.

Later, when I prepared his dinner, Ted announced that he would no longer eat with me because I had obviously been poisoning his food.

We were entering a new phase of the madness. Accusations against me that had been subtle and merely suggested before were now direct and open.

Ted was sure he was being poisoned. Every twinge, every cramp, every headache however slight, meant that the arsenic was accumulating in his body. Slowly he would become disabled, impotent, weak, and disoriented, and then the

Commies would move in for the kill. He began eating only a few bites of food each meal, merely enough to stave off hunger, or else he would ignore the dinner completely and fill up on fruit and crackers.

Once, when he came to the table and refused his plate, I switched it with my own. The triumph of reason. The ultimate proof. But Ted wouldn't touch either one.

"They're both poisoned," he explained, "only the Communists have given you an antidote to neutralize the effects."

How had they been giving me this antidote?

In the water supply.

Then why wouldn't Ted be drinking it also?

Because they had a device that puts an antidote in the water when I turned on the faucet, but not when Ted touched it.

And how, God help us, did they know whether it was Ted's hand or mine on the faucet?

The bathroom was bugged. There was a microphone inside the roll of toilet paper, probably. The mirror itself was one-way glass.

That meant the Communists were camping in our medicine chest, maybe?

They can do anything. They'll stop at nothing.

Despite my resolution to avoid arguing with Ted, it was impossible to stay detached. He insisted on being heard. My silence infuriated him. He followed me about from room to room, repeating the same monologue endlessly. His life was wasted, but he had so much to give. Why had this happened to him? Why did I let it happen? Why didn't we leave him alone so that he could contribute something to the world? What had he done that made us want to rob him of ambition and success? No matter what his problem, it seemed, someone else was invariably to blame.

I tried getting out of the apartment. I began walking to

the library daily, or sat at the back of a nearby church to write. But I was uneasy away from him for long, and arrived home one afternoon to find him sitting on the couch, somewhat disoriented, with a crumpled necktie in one hand. He had tried to hang himself from the shower stall, he told me, but it hadn't worked.

I stuffed the tie in the incinerator as though that would be the end of the problem, as though there weren't a dozen more, plus belts and blind cords, at his disposal. My legs felt weak, and I lay down on the bed. I was home now, and he would not try it again. But tomorrow or the next day? And all the while I fought it, the awful thought returned that it would be so simple if I could just come home to find him dead. The problems would all be over. How was it possible that so much trouble and turbulence was wrapped up in one man, that one human being—one bunch of bones, sinew, and veins—could affect my life so profoundly and make me so unhappy? I could not leave the house again without being aware of this fearful wish. Was this trip really necessary? Or did I hope, just under the civilized surface, that it would be all over when I returned?

Had he been continuously sarcastic and belligerent, it would have been easy to think of leaving. But his periods of bitterness alternated with genuine terror, in which his words came fast and breathlessly, he perspired, fidgeted, and clutched me to him, begging me not to leave. He would talk about getting help, of knowing that he was ill, but he felt it was a physical illness, induced by the doctors themselves. He would remember trips we had taken together, plans we had made, and cry when he realized how few of the dreams had come true. But by afternoon or evening he would be hard-eyed and cynical again.

I tried to focus on the part of him that was in touch with reality and ignore the rest. I rewarded him when he talked rationally by being warm and responsive, and ignored him, or tried to, when he talked nonsense. In desperation, I thought perhaps I could reach his subconscious while he slept at night, and after he had fallen asleep, I whispered in his ear:

"You're sick, Ted. Your sickness makes you suspicious of everyone, but your wife and the doctors are your friends. No one wants to hurt you. That's your imagination. You must trust someone in order to get well."

Brave new world. For three nights I went through this highly unscientific ritual before it fell apart. On the fourth night, Ted sat straight up in bed and stared at me. "You're trying to brainwash me, aren't you? The Commies put you up to this."

There is something about the middle of the night that brings out the demons in us all. There is something about the hours between two and four that induces a disproportionate amount of worry. Fears that seem manageable in the light of day take on gigantic proportions in the dark of a silent bedroom. And so, when Ted managed to fall asleep, it was sometimes I who lay awake and fought the rising panic, imagining the worst so I could deal with it if it happened .

How long, I would wonder, before Ted turned on me completely? How long before I awoke to find him standing with a belt not around his own throat but mine? At what point does conversation give way and gibberish take over? How long before the mind snapped entirely and the man ran amuck? Was I really prepared for the possibility of walking in the door and finding that he had killed himself in my absence? Would I scream? Would I kneel and touch his body? Would I be overwhelmed by grief? Or would it be gratitude?

What, in fact, hurt the most about his psychosis? Sorrow

100

for him—for the terror and the pain and panic that ate at him continually? Sorrow for myself? The fact that dreams were destroyed, time wasted, that love and trust had been replaced by suspicion? Or was it the stigma of having an insane husband that I could not bear? How does one explain a man who was doing so well? What other big change had come into his life in the last few years except marriage, and wasn't this, then—in the eyes of friends and relatives—proof enough that I was not only incapable of making a man happy but of keeping him sane?

If only I could attribute his sickness to the war. That was respectable—noble, even. A man goes off to war and comes home disabled in the head; pity and gratitude, that's what such a man would get, and his wife as well. Could the bombing raids over Germany have affected the gray matter? Was the cerebellum damaged somehow by changes in altitude? Was perception altered by the roar of engines, and wasn't it possible that the stress of the whole experience had proved just too much for his fragile system and had begun a slow erosion, only to appear—like rust—at some time in the future?

Perhaps the war had affected us both. While Ted was taking off on flights from England, I was an eleven-year-old girl in saddle shoes looking at posters of Uncle Sam with one finger over his lips. "Loose lips sink ships," the caption warned.

I was tearing out stamps from my ration books, saving tinfoil (for what, I never really knew), planting a victory garden, and cowering in the darkness on nights the city practiced a blackout. I went to Armistice Day programs at school where the science teacher solemnly recited "In Flanders fields . . ." and by the time he'd said "the poppies blow," at least a dozen girls were crying. Some wept in earnest. I never dreamed that the man I would marry was at that moment zipping himself into a flight suit.

101

It was even earlier, in fact, when I was eight or nine, that the fears of Hitler had first begun—when I lay in the darkness and thought of stories I'd heard about the storm troopers ripping small babies in half, bashing their heads on the curb, or forcing Jews to kneel down and lick up their own spittle. I had imagined the sound of their boots on the street outside, the breaking down of our door, and how they would swarm through the house taking all our food. One evening I had even crept downstairs and stuffed a piece of bread in the well of the pencil sharpener. They would never look there. Family Saved From Starvation by Cleverness of Younger Daughter. . . .

But there was no way to connect Ted's present condition with the war, and I knew it. And so, having gone through the mental calisthenics of clutching at one excuse and then another, I would escape next into a world of words where the very impersonality of clinical descriptions tricked me into believing that the problems were manageable. Beginning with Dr. Pollard's "one small corner of Ted's personality," I would think of all I had ever read about marriage and schizophrenia, of phrases so void of emotion and feeling that we were people no longer, but a mere case study. Ted and I became—in this jargon of noninvolvement—an anesthetized "unit." My exasperated shrieks of rage and frustration when Ted goaded me to the breaking point became clinical "expressions of hostility." Ted's delusions of torture and murder were transformed on the printed page to "the patient's inability to distinguish psychotic thought from material reality." My emotional flights from the house to escape those delusions were simply a "defense mechanism" and my fear of what I might find on my return was the result, in part, of "manifest guilt." By reading such books and reciting such phrases, I made Ted and me pawns on a chessboard instead of people, and our problems were mere textbook puzzles, to be solved during the course of the semester.

But I could not escape for long. Twice Ted went to see a psychiatrist whom Dr. Pollard had recommended in Minnesota, but the doctor refused to take him as a patient unless he were admitted to a hospital, and Ted would have none of it. I wondered about the possibility of committing him, but on what basis? Could I get three doctors to testify that he was incompetent to handle his own affairs, when all we could prove was that he was out of work? Were we so naïve as to think that when he appeared for his hearing, if he appeared at all, he would oblige us by enumerating the fears that would commit him?

Tearfully I plunked myself down in the Family Service Bureau and told a counselor my story. Ted was an intelligent man going to waste, the marriage had little left for either of us, and somebody had to do something. Would they please help?

I hated the reply she gave me, yet it began the slow process of breaking away from Ted which was necessary for my own health.

"What do you want us to do?" the counselor asked patiently. "Do you want us to force your husband to see a doctor and to stay in treatment? Do you really think we can do that?"

I realized that that's what I was asking, and that it was impossible.

Arguments at the apartment became more intense as I began to voice my own opinions, my own needs. There were days when our apartment was filled with tension, rising voices, anger and frustration. Once, when I felt I could no longer take the accusations, the sarcasm, the self-pity, I lunged at Ted in the middle of his tirade, scratching at his face with my nails, crying, wild with fury. He shoved me back, and, as I collapsed in a chair, surprised and sobbing, he surveyed me coldly from across the room.

"You're sick," he said. "You're mentally ill. You need help."

There was a knock on the door, and Ted answered. There stood two young Mormon missionaries. They looked as terrified as I felt within myself, and stammered that they had been sent by a mutual friend. Ted closed the door on them.

"You're sick," he said again, concentrating on me. "You're out of control."

I wondered if it were possible. After all, I would be the last to know. What if all this time I had been as sick as Ted and not known it? What if much of what Ted had said was true? What if there *were* active Communists at the University? Perhaps Ted had once been a member of an organization he hadn't told me about, and perhaps he *did* know too much. Perhaps there *had* been subtle threats, warning him to leave, and perhaps this had triggered his madness. Perhaps by refusing to believe anything at all which he had told me, I was shutting out part of the truth. Perhaps I was indeed the mad one, and getting sicker. What kind of woman would lunge at her husband like that, scratching and clawing like some rabid animal? Perhaps it was I who was destined for the ultimate breakdown.

I went back to the church where I had often sat in the back pew writing, and this time I talked with the assistant pastor. He did not ask about my faith or my lack of it, he did not care that neither Ted nor I had ever attended or contributed anything at all, he did not care that he was another in a long list of people who had tried without success to help, he did not even suggest that we pray. I was in

104

pain, emotional pain, and he told me I could call him any time, day or night, it made no difference. He offered himself as my rock, my safety net, and he was one of several people who helped me stay sane. Dear Charles Sweet, did you or any of the other people who were so kind ever know what you meant to me?

February came, forcing a decision. On this particular day Ted had been restless, unusually agitated, cynical, and belligerent. He ate nothing at all, and seemed on the verge of a critical decision. In the middle of the afternoon, he said he was leaving, stuffed a few things in his suitcase, denounced me loudly, and left. Did I feel relief? Some, perhaps. But at seven, I was in the kitchen cleaning up the dishes when I heard him come back. As soon as I turned and faced him, I knew he was different. Somehow I sensed that there had been a change in his eyes, his perception, his metabolism even, as though he had gone through a complete metamorphosis, for the worse.

It was I, however, who must have seemed transformed. He stared at me as though seeing me for the first time.

"What's the matter, Ted?"

He did not answer, but continued to stare. He walked a few steps to one side, then the other, his face breaking into a strange smile of recognition.

I was uneasy. When he still did not answer, I put down the dish towel and attempted to walk into the living room. As I brushed past him, he suddenly shoved me hard away from him, sending me reeling against the wall.

"I know who you are!" he said, the strange smile turning into anger. "I know who you are now, *Mother*."

He enunciated the last word with a precision and bitterness that bespoke a universe of hatred.

"Do you really think you can go on disguising yourself?"

he continued, walking slowly toward me again. "All these years . . . I should have known. . . ."

"Ted, I am not your mother."

He ignored me. "*Now* I know what you're up to. *Now* I begin to see you for what you really are, *Mother.*"

His lips curled whenever he said the word, his face was contorted, and I genuinely feared for my life.

I went into the bedroom and Ted followed. He began taking blankets off the bed along with his pillow and announced that he would not sleep with me again. Oedipus and Jocasta. I locked the bedroom door after him, the first time I had ever considered doing so, and knew that the marriage, for all practical, pleasurable purposes, was over. Tomorrow I would leave.

The next morning, Ted could not remember what had driven him out on the couch except that I had been "acting strangely" as he put it.

It wasn't enough. I had been waiting for an incident, and perhaps this was all I was going to get. I told Ted I could no longer live like this, and he agreed. He said that he had come to a decision himself: it was a mistake to have come to Minnesota. It was a mistake to run away. He realized he was sick. He could not separate reality from fantasy. He wanted to go back home and see Dr. Pollard. In fact, he planned to ask whether the doctor had room now on his schedule to see him regularly, and when he made the phone call, Dr. Pollard said yes.

"It was a mistake" was becoming a household phrase. But we believe what we wish to believe, and I wished to believe in Ted. Going home seemed to be the answer we were looking for. He would enter therapy with the doctor he had trusted, I would see about getting my teaching job again. We would go back to confront those fears, and would simply write off the Minnesota experiment as a bad joke. Sanity, here we come.

There was very little money left and I did not want to waste it moving a truckload of furniture. We decided to sell everything but the piano and our books which we would put in storage, and send for them when we were sure of a new address. We filled the Studebaker with our remaining possessions and on a frigid late afternoon set out for the Big City.

Was it the Biblical injunction about turning the other cheek that made me do it? Or the admonition to forgive him seventy times seven? Did I think that if I could just get him back home and onto the Pollard couch as a bona fide twice-a-week patient, recovery was imminent? Or did I trust because it was the easiest immediate solution and I desperately needed to lean on someone else?

Fifty miles out of town, Ted changed his mind. What were we doing? Why were we going back to the place where he had been so unhappy? What potion had I put in his coffee that made him agree to such a wild plot? Was Dr. Pollard in on it too? Would the Commies be there waiting in the doctor's office to abduct him when he arrived? We were all a pack of wolves, he said. We were all in on the scheme, and there wasn't a soul in the world he could really trust. . . . He swung the car around and headed north again.

I said absolutely nothing. My world had suddenly grown very small. I no longer looked forward to plans and dreams to make me happy. My pleasure consisted entirely of the here and now. I wanted only to get a hot bath, eat a warm supper, and sleep. I was overwhelmed suddenly with the desire to escape.

For twenty-five miles I remained silent while Ted enumerated all the reasons why we should not have sold the furniture and left the apartment. Then, halfway back again, he changed his mind. Perhaps we should go through with it after all. Dr. Pollard was expecting him. Maybe he should turn around and head south. What did I think?

And then, this human sponge, this lump of jelly, this living mattress who had scarcely done a thing in her own defense through six and a half years of marriage, opened her mouth and said, "No, Ted, I'm staying in Minnesota. Keep going."

I could hardly believe it myself.

Ted was apologetic, angry with himself for being so indecisive. He begged me to go back with him. He wanted me, needed me, could not live without me. . . . I wanted a hot bath, needed a warm supper, and could not live without sleep.

"Take me back to town," I said, "and if you're really serious about seeing Dr. Pollard and starting again, you go on alone."

Ted pulled off the road to talk it over. He said he was sure now. He would not change his mind again. But I was retreating fast into my escape world of nothingness. My mind shut him out. My feet were cold. The sky was gray and getting grayer.

"I'm not going," I said. "If you find an apartment down there and start treatment, then I'll come."

We headed north again and arrived in town late. Ted got a kitchenette apartment for me in a rundown hotel that had weekly and monthly rates. He helped me carry in the clothes, a box of kitchen utensils, and my writing materials. He sat down a few minutes to get warm, cried, promised to do his best, and finally, at two A.M., at nine above zero, left.

I awoke the next morning in the efficiency apartment to see it for the first time in the light of day. The two dirty windows overlooked a junkyard next door, and a carillon in the distance chimed out an elegant tune every hour that floated incongruously over the scrap metal. I had a double bed, a dresser, a table, two chairs, and a small stove-sink-refrigerator combination. The bathroom consisted of sink and toilet. The tub, alas, was down the hall in a communal women's lounge. I would bathe, I decided, by buying a large plastic laundry basket and filling it with water from my sink.

An assortment of footsteps and coughs drifted in now and then from the hallway. Someone tried the handle of my door and then moved on. I lay as if in a cocoon and attempted to look at my life objectively. I was alone now, really alone. The hotel was seedy and cheap, but it was warm, and if I ate sparingly, I could live on the little I earned from my writing. We had about twelve hundred dollars left in a joint bank account, but Ted would need that if he got an apartment back home and began treatment. I would live in my little hovel writing till I earned enough money to pay for a semester at the local college. Now the writing was for real—for survival.

I had never really considered writing for a living before. It was always a hobby, an escape, an immensely satisfying excursion. I never saw myself as bookish. There was something perverse in my eyes about a person who sat in a garret all day twiddling with words instead of living out life in the flesh. But here I was at twenty-four, begging to be shut away for a while, to be protected from life, eager to have done with people and to spend my time with sentences instead.

I got up and dressed, called Charles Sweet to tell him where I was and what had happened. It helped to recite my plans aloud, to make them sound official, to get the Methodist seal of approval, perhaps. Then I took the bus to the college, picked up a catalogue, bought some groceries and came home.

Ted was sitting on the bed when I walked in, and my

little bubble burst. I felt more alone when he was there than when he was gone. When he was away, myself and I were friends. We talked to each other aloud, in soothing, comforting tones. When he was there, both of us together could not handle him.

He was cold, he told me. Almost frozen. He had spent the night in the car. He was hungry and needed sleep. I fed him, and he stayed in bed for two days. My garret had been invaded. I was in limbo again.

The indecision about going or staying incapacitated him. He wanted me to decide for him. I refused. For the next two months he would declare he was going back home and would be gone for three days, and then return, confessing that he had merely slept in the car. He looked thin and sick, and had caught a cold. Weeks dragged on.

And then one afternoon he came in, surly and indignant. "They" had thought up still another plot against him. He had just turned a corner, he said, when someone flagged him down and told him he had struck an elderly woman. Ted had walked back to the corner to find an old lady sitting on the curb. She told bystanders that the Studebaker had rounded the corner so sharply it had come up over the curb and struck her heel, knocking her down. Anyone could see, Ted said, that it was just a story and that she was an accomplished actress. He had read about this racket before. People did it to collect huge payments from insurance companies, but obviously "they" wanted him in jail.

I sat down on the bed, my legs trembling. I felt personally responsible for the injury. I alone had known how carelessly Ted had been driving, how ill he really was. At this moment he seemed to me more psychotic than he had ever been, for he showed no remorse, no concern, no sympathy—only anger that he was the accused.

"What happened then, Ted?"

"A policeman came and made a report."

I knew that Ted would have to be committed now. I called Dr. Pollard and asked him to recommend the best hospital in the country. He said there were several, but two that were outstanding: the Mayo Clinic in Rochester, and a private sanitarium, in Maryland. The Sanitarium, he said, often took patients deemed hopeless everywhere else.

I wrote Mayo Clinic because it was closest. There would be no beds for six months, they replied. The Sanitarium wrote that they would have a bed within a month, but they would not take a patient without first interviewing both him and his family. Then I called Mr. Moreno in Albuquerque and told him about his son.

No one treats the bearer of bad news kindly, and I could not blame Ted's father for his lack of enthusiasm. I explained how we had set out for the Big City and turned back. I told him about Ted's striking the old woman and Dr. Pollard's suggestions. I asked him to help me take Ted to Maryland for an interview. He said he would come.

Between us, we persuaded Ted to go. Somehow we got him on the plane for Washington, then into a taxi for the twelve-mile ride out to the suburbs where the wind was warm and flowers were blooming, and it seemed like a whole new world waiting to cure somebody.

As the cab pulled up the long drive, lined with oak trees, Ted remarked that the main building looked like something out of a Charles Addams cartoon, and that there were undoubtedly torture devices in the basement. Mr. Moreno added that it certainly didn't look like any kind of hospital to him, and what did we really know about it anyway? What had we ever known about Dr. Pollard, in fact? Didn't all Ted's troubles begin when he went to see that psychiatrist

111

instead of listening to his parents? What could a psychiatrist have done for him that the Morenos couldn't? Doctors were all a bunch of Commies who had messed up his son.

And on this note of confidence and trust, we paid the driver and went up the steps to the front door.

FIVE

THE MAIN BUILDING at the Sanitarium looked, indeed, like the mansion of a moderately prosperous Marylander. The drive looped around in front of it, around a little island thick with trees which blocked the view of the door from the street. Steps led up to the front patio, lined with potted shrubs, to the big white door itself.

Inside, a hallway divided a small receptionist's room on the right from a comfortable living room on the left. Beyond these were offices for the doctors and social workers. I knew nothing more about the place except that Dr. Pollard had recommended it, and that treatment was by psychotherapy only, without the use of drugs or shock.

A pleasant receptionist took our name, and an administrative doctor ushered Ted to his office for the initial interview. I was instantly impressed with the personal touches. There were no impatient, overworked nurses scurrying in and out, no names being called out over the loudspeaker, no rattle of pans and trays by unthinking attendants, no dreary institutional look about the building, inside or out. The atmosphere was comfortably quiet. The air smelled fresh. Birds called to one another from the dozens of tall trees that surrounded the place, and I felt this just had to be it.

While Ted was seeing the doctor, Mr. Moreno and I were taken to the comptroller's office. He was a soft-spoken gentleman, a retired colonel, who asked us about the flight, the weather in Minnesota versus Maryland, and told us a brief history of the Sanitarium, making a point of the fact that it was a private institution, and that the fees were considered, by some, to be high.

"How much will it cost?" Mr. Moreno asked flatly, impatient with the sidestepping.

"Two thousand a month," came the answer.

We sat stunned. A *month!* More than Ted and I had in our entire savings! Who on earth could afford such treatment? I had only been earning $4,500 a year on my last job!

"Two thousand a month!" Mr. Moreno sputtered. "I'm not a rich man!"

I realized I should have asked this very basic question before we came. We were out of our class. Only the wealthiest people in America could afford to come here. I was embarrassed even to be sitting in the office.

The colonel was embarrassed too, for us. "Sometimes," he said hesitantly, as though he was not supposed to divulge this information, "we reduce the fee for families who just can't afford that much. If the doctors feel that the patient might achieve outpatient status rather quickly, they will sometimes accept a patient of lower economic limits, and then, when the patient is switched to outpatient status, the cost comes down. But we do not like to accept patients unless

114

the family is in a position to afford at least two years of treatment."

I knew it was impossible. Mr. Moreno was already standing up, turning his hat around and around by the brim as he waited for me in the doorway. And when we were taken next for a preliminary interview with the admitting doctor, I could not hide my disappointment. Breathlessly, almost frantically, I told him that the Sanitarium was our last hope. I described all that we had gone through in the preceding two years, how highly Dr. Pollard had recommended the place, how hard I would work to help pay for the treatment, and offered, in effect, blood, sweat, toil, and tears if only they would take Ted at a price we could afford.

The doctor was gentle and thoroughly humane. He had seen the scene played out, no doubt, many times before. He agreed that Ted was certainly more in contact with reality than many of the patients there, that—as far as paranoid schizophrenia went—his prognosis might be better than some, but that we also must remember that the disease itself, in all the patients who manifested it, was a difficult one to break through. He would agree, however, to take Ted, if we could support him in at least one year of inpatient therapy and another year of outpatient treatment. It was possible they could do very little for him during this time, but there was also the hope that they could. He was willing to reduce inpatient costs to sixteen hundred dollars per month in our case and outpatient costs to six hundred when Ted was ready. But it was unfair to a patient, he said, to admit him for only a few months and then, after he had established trust with the doctors and aides, to have to terminate his therapy because the family couldn't afford any more.

We would have to go back to Minnesota and think about

115

it, I told the doctor, knowing it was out of the question. Could we let him know later?

Certainly.

We met Ted in the living room again, and walked silently out the big front door to wait for the cab. Once outside, I buried my head against Ted and cried like a small girl, big aching sobs that I seemed to have saved up for many months, and Ted put his arm around me and stroked my hair. A passing nurse observed us briefly and nodded sympathetically to Ted. Mr. Moreno stood by with his face frozen, unnerved by this sudden outburst from a daughter-in-law he did not really know. As the cab pulled up the drive, he remarked that he had "some" money, but not that much, and that it was too bad we didn't have a rich uncle.

But we did! As a matter of fact, I had two of them. All the way to the hotel in Washington, I thought about it, my head swimming. Did I dare ask, when they scarcely knew Ted? It was not like asking for a loan of five hundred dollars. This was a fantastic amount of money which, in the end, might prove to have gained nothing at all. They wouldn't even get a share of the profits! I thought of the time they had been robbed of a huge orange crane by the black sheep of the clan, and wondered if they would be willing to loan me the price of even one small bulldozer. We would need to guarantee the Sanitarium a total of over twenty-six thousand dollars.

Back in the hotel room, I told Mr. Moreno my plan. He said that if my uncles would agree to put up ten thousand, he would put up another ten, and I said that somehow I would pay the rest. I was excited. Mr. Moreno was glum. Ted was uneasy. While I made the long distance call to my parents, Ted went out for a walk and Mr. Moreno took a nap.

It is unfair to ask others to do our unpleasant tasks. My

parents should have told me to ask my uncles myself, but they didn't. I told Mother where we were, what had happened, and asked if she could call her brothers and request a ten-thousand-dollar loan. She was speechless. My father came on the line. Yes, he said, they would ask. It was an embarrassing situation, and I was putting them in a difficult position, but they would ask and let me know in a few days. Meanwhile, there was something they suggested I do.

I listened. It seemed they had heard of a famous faith healer somewhere in Pennsylvania who had the marvelous ability to cure by laying his hands on the afflicted. Before I went back to Minnesota, they wanted me to look up this saint and have him try his luck on Ted. It may be that this would solve everything, and the ten thousand would not be needed.

To understand this request, you must understand my parents. They were neither religious fanatics nor uneducated fools. But they believed intensely in divine intervention. If there were any possibility that this man was a sage, as they had heard, not a charlatan, why not give it a try?

My father was the son of a country preacher and a practical nurse who was midwife to dozens of babies in the surrounding hills. He grew up steeped in the church, more so, perhaps, than he cared to be, but nonetheless attended a church in Atlanta as a young bachelor where he met my mother. After their marriage they attended a religious college in Indiana where my father studied for the ministry, but gave it up a year before graduation to enter the world of business. My mother graduated with a degree in religious education.

We grew up, then, in a church-centered home in which most of our leisure time was focused on church activities. Along with the Mark Twain that our parents read us at night, or the poems of James Whitcomb Riley, Egermeier's voluminous *Bible Story Book,* all 233 stories, was the main course. It took almost a full year to get through it, and once we reached the end, where the disciples scattered unto the far corners of the earth, Mother turned back to Adam and Eve and started it all over again. We heard it in its entirety at least three or four times. We were indoctrinated in Bible drills, in which Mother would call out the number of a chapter and verse, and we would scramble madly through our gold-leafed pages to see who could find and read it first.

I came to know Jacob and Esau as intimately as if I had grown up with them. I knew the ten plagues and what Saul saw on the road to Damascus. I knew who had begat whom and which sons were doomed to suffer even unto the fourth generation. I learned that I could read of unspeakable things, lightly passed over by Mrs. Egermeier, by looking them up in the Bible firsthand.

Itinerant preachers, faith healers, and layers-on-of-hands were not unknown to us even then. As small girls, my sister and I spent long hours playing "revival," and somehow it was always I who was chosen as sinner. When we were older we lived next door to a fanatical woman who insisted on taking her children to seven nights of revival services every summer. Each evening her oldest boys would climb high in our maple tree to escape, and after prodding futilely at them with a clothes pole, Mrs. Baumgarten would suggest that my sister and I go in their place. We always went. There was something about the tent out in the clover field, the sawdust floor, the portable organ, and the preacher in the white suit that was hypnotic. Each summer, then, for one week, we were saved nightly, and went tearfully up to the front of the tent to kneel with the weeping red-eyed women who greeted us as sisters in iniquity. Mary Magdalene, that was me.

But that's not all. I was a respected member of the Loyal

Temperance League, and sat entranced with the other children as we watched a demonstration of a raw egg dissolving in pure alcohol, having been told that this was what beer did to the lining of the stomach.

There were questions, though, that no one seemed eager to answer. The answers I did get were often contradictory. God was described as being either so powerful that he could do anything He wished, or impotent, because He had given us free choice and therefore was powerless to intervene in our own mistakes. Because of Adam and Eve's fall (wasn't that an awfully long time to hold a grudge?) we ourselves were responsible for wars and famines and the butchering of little babies. Yet with the proper spirit, the right prayers, and faith the size of a mustard seed, we might persuade Him to help us out on occasion. Sometimes He intervened, it seemed, without even being asked. And sometimes, though the entire congregation got down on its knees, God remained absolutely deaf. Just one of the mysteries we would find out after we got to heaven.

Inherent in the Christian faith, however, is guilt, and the chronic, nagging suspicion that perhaps one's faith does not even measure up to a mustard seed. Though my parents had never been particularly impressed with preachers who claimed marvelous powers, they felt, perhaps, that their faith —theirs and mine—was being tested by Ted's illness, and it might be possible that a pilgrimage of sorts to Pennsylvania would convince God we meant business, and induce Him to cast out the demon.

As my mind whirled about this unexpected suggestion, the questions came hurtling back. If God indeed had the power to heal, where had He been for the last two years? If we were being punished, somehow, Ted and I, what about that poor old woman on the Minnesota street corner who had nothing to do with it at all? If anyone should have a

119

direct pipeline to God, it was Mrs. Moreno herself, yet she couldn't seem to pull off the miracle either. What sort of celestial insecurity was it, anyway, that would make God refuse to lift His little finger till we all fell down on our knees and called Him Lord and Master? Why the necessity for begging and pleading when He was all-knowing and knew exactly what needed to be done? And after all we had been through in the last two years, God Omnipotent wanted me to rent a car now and haul Ted to a faith healer in the next state when I couldn't even keep him in a hotel room?

No, I said. I couldn't possibly do it. If I wouldn't do my part, my father replied, how could I expect anyone else to help me? The phone call ended with tension on both sides.

There were some things, I found, that I could no longer discuss with my parents. It was not only the physical distance between us when I left Oakton that made us seem strangers. The span itself became filled with experiences that could not be shared. In a search for religious truth we had come up with radically different answers, and while I was satisfied to admit that I did not know anything for sure, my parents were eager to fill these voids with certainties which had proved comforting to them. But I could not accept this comfort, and it hurt because of the pain it caused them. I must have seemed hopelessly arrogant.

Mr. Moreno awoke an hour later. Ted had still not come back from his walk. We grew increasingly uneasy. We had no knowledge of Washington, no car, and our plane was due to leave early the next morning. Where and how would we begin to look for Ted?

The hours ticked on and Mr. Moreno was wretched. He should never have come, never have taken a nap, never have let his son out of his sight. Singly we went out to look for Ted while the other remained in the room and waited. At ten o'clock the door opened and Ted came in. He took off his shoes and lay down on the bed, staring straight up at the ceiling, refusing to talk. At last, after an exasperating twenty minutes, he told us. He had tried to buy a gun and see the President.

In Minnesota the next day, my mother called. My uncles had agreed to lend me a maximum of ten thousand dollars, to be paid in monthly sums toward Ted's hospitalization. Jubilantly I called the Sanitarium and the doctor said that they would have a place for Ted by the middle of June. Only one month to wait.

I was filled with both gratitude and reassurance. Ted would have the best help available in the country—the best doctors, the most skillful nurses, the kindest hospital environment. Ted, with his fine mind, was sure to make it. Wasn't he?

The problem with doctors is that we put them on pedestals and refuse to let them down. The doctors at the Sanitarium had not given me a guarantee. They did not even speak in percentages. What they offered me was cautious hope, and because I was starving for reassurance, I gulped it down and considered the contract sealed.

Mr. Moreno was less elated. Maryland was a long way off. Sixteen hundred dollars a month—half from my uncles and half from his own pocket—was a lot of money. What if Ted was "cured" but Mr. M. didn't like what he turned out to be? What, in other words, would the Morenos get out of all this besides a so-called well-adjusted son? What about filial gratitude? What about obedience and respect? What about reverence for authority?

I had thought Ted might be pleased, since he had seemed to like the Sanitarium. I had thought he would at least appreciate all we were doing. I had forgotten already the ambivalence of the past two years. Ted received the news of my uncles' loan with extreme agitation. How could we justify spending all that money on him? How could we ever pay it off? What if it didn't work, and he was no better than he was now?

These were legitimate questions which I had preferred not to face. I felt we had no choice. We had tried everything else. But the questions were insurmountable for Ted. That evening he got in his car and drove off, a day before his father was to go back to Albuquerque. When he did not come back by morning, I called Mr. Moreno at his hotel and he canceled his flight.

Days went on, with no word from Ted. I was both angry and frightened. Mr. Moreno came over for an hour each morning and again in the afternoon, and we sat glumly in my dingy one-room flat speculating on where Ted might have gone. I checked his things again for a clue. He had taken no clothes, no toilet articles. Then I discovered that a bottle of sleeping pills was missing.

There are situations in which our deepest fears are half hopes. How simple things would be if Ted took those pills, the whole bottle. No more decisions and revisions which a moment could reverse. No necessity for a loan from my reluctant uncles. No more dreams that never got off the ground. I would be a young widow and could begin a new life. I flogged myself for the thought.

The druggist told me that even if Ted should swallow the entire contents, they would not kill him but rather put him to sleep for a day or two; they were not as powerful as a prescription drug. We were not reassured. What if he swallowed them all and continued driving? What of the road winding along the bluffs above the Mississippi?

We began checking hospitals. We notified the police. Beyond that there was nothing we could do but wait. I hoped that whatever happened was already over. The guilty fantasy of Ted sinking down in the muddy waters of the river, gasping for breath, tortured me. As the wait grew longer yet, I forgot him as he was at his most exasperating, and remembered the tender moments instead, the gentleness, the passion, and then I began to long for him, and the torture was refined still further.

At the beginning of the second week, an insurance agent knocked on the door to say that the elderly woman whom Ted had struck with the Studebaker had been operated on for a broken hip. Could he please speak to my husband?

It was not helpful to our credit rating to reply that my husband had disappeared. The agent found it unconvincing. Mr. Moreno, an insurance agent himself, was mortified, and talked of going back to New Mexico. "Ted made his own bed," he said at least once a day, "now he has to lie in it."

As the second week came to an end, I found it increasingly difficult to sleep at all. If Ted had committed suicide, we should have heard something by now. A Studebaker does not disappear so easily. And if he were alive, he might run over someone else, or try again to buy a gun. Charles Sweet came by frequently to sit with me and talk. Just to pass the time. Just quiet concern. It was good to talk with someone who was sane.

And then, at the beginning of the third week, the communal phone in the hallway rang at one in the morning, and I knew beyond doubt that it was for me. I threw on a robe and rushed toward it.

It was the sheriff in La Crosse, Wisconsin. He had found Ted sitting on the courthouse steps, confused and disoriented, and had given him some soup and put him to bed. Would I please come after him?

Why, I wonder, did I greet the news with immense relief —hope, even? What made me so eager to start the turmoil all over again? Why, in fact, did I feel compelled to call

123

Mr. Moreno at once, disturbing his sleep, and suggest we get on the train immediately for La Crosse? Ted had inconvenienced us for two weeks, yet while he slept at the sheriff's quarters, we were rushing about to catch a train at two in the morning. The prodigal son was about to get the fatted calf treatment, and if I could have afforded a bevy of violinists, I imagine I would have taken them along. Love is a strange thing, and love mixed with immaturity and loneliness, with guilt and naïveté, is stranger still.

It was five in the morning when we got to La Crosse. Ted looked like a resident of the Bowery. His clothes were dirty and wrinkled and he had a growth of beard. His face was pale and he seemed upset to have been wakened. The sheriff suggested he might like to shave before we left, and lent him an electric razor. Then he sat down beside us while the drone of the razor buzzed from the bathroom.

"I'm no psychiatrist," the sheriff said, "but I think this young man is mentally ill. Men like this shouldn't be driving around. You ought to put him in a hospital."

The accusatory tone. Didn't I care? Did I think this was normal? How dare I let him wander about the streets making a nuisance of himself?

If he were a Great Dane, I could have tied him up. If he were a cat, I could have locked him in the house. But because he was a man, I had no choice, it seemed, except to wait until society decided it had had enough and took him from me.

"Let's go back, Ted," I said, when he came out.

Ted said nothing. Absolutely nothing. He put on his shoes slowly, fumbling with the knots, picked up his jacket, studied his face in the mirror, ignored the sheriff's extended hand, and followed me outside.

Once inside the Studebaker, however, Ted became sullen,

then surly, and finally belligerent. Why didn't we leave him alone? Why did we have to follow him about the country? What right had we to interfere with his life? Why not let him die quickly and get it over with, instead of shipping him off to a sanitarium for the slow torture and certain death that awaited him there? Were we trusted relatives or accomplices in the plot?

As Ted became louder, his father—having been awakened in the middle of the night himself—was no model of patience. Together we tried to explain that the sheriff had called us, that the insurance agent had visited us, that Ted was our responsibility, and that we could not separate ourselves from him that easily.

Ted listened but he did not hear. He drove aimlessly around the streets, passing the courthouse for the fifth time. He would not go back to Minnesota. He hadn't asked the sheriff to call. He had no desire to see either of us, no desire to live. Just get out, he said, leave him alone, and he would make sure next time that he was never found. And then he began a long, bitter denunciation of his father, his homelife, his childhood. . . .

It took only seconds to provoke Mr. Moreno into a rage. The car reverberated with name-calling, stamping feet, pounding on the dashboard, yells. And suddenly, when Ted stopped at a light, his father got out and announced his refusal to ride any further with such a despicable ingrate. He refused to say the word "son." He wanted me to get out also, but I couldn't. If I did, the next call might be from Indiana or Texas, and I would have it to do all over again. Better to face it now. Ted roared off at the change of the light, leaving his father there in his beige summer suit and wide-brimmed hat, his face gray with fury, his lips trembling. It was not yet six in the morning.

125

For an hour, in the early dawn, we drove around the streets, Ted mumbling angrily, turning his accusations to me. What was in it for me? Why didn't I get out and leave him forever? I have often wondered why I didn't. It was my chance. Mr. Moreno would have been my witness. Hadn't I done my best, all I could? We could have separated so easily, and I would have left with no forwarding address.

But one does not escape a marriage as simply as that, and we do inexplicable things when we are lonely.

I knew that in his warped way, Ted felt he was doing the best thing for me. What would I have done if I thought that Ted was borrowing ten thousand dollars senselessly, for a cure that wouldn't take? What would I have done if I knew that every day I was alive I was causing trouble for somebody? What would I have done if I'd felt myself in an impossible situation with no means of escape?

But I knew Ted too well to believe that this mood would last forever. In a few days—a few hours, even—he would be terrified again. It was his illness, I knew, that was ranting at me, not the Ted I once loved. If it were I, would I have wanted him to leave me, just when help was only two weeks away?

And so I stayed, and when a patrol car approached on the deserted street, I leaned over, pressed the horn down, and held it.

"Stop it!" Ted hissed, and tried to push my hand away, but I held on. The horn cut through the early morning stillness, an incredibly loud blast.

"Stop it!" Ted yelled, and swore.

The squad car made a U-turn and signaled him to pull over.

The officer looked in the window, his eyes quickly scanning the seat, the floor, our hands. . . .

126

"You folks having some trouble?"

"Yes," I said quickly. "My husband is mentally ill. He needs help."

Ted sat like a sphinx, staring straight ahead, furious.

The policeman looked closely at Ted, then at me. He turned toward the second officer back in the cruiser and shook his head slightly. *A couple of dingbats,* the shake seemed to say.

"Okay," he said. "You want to follow me in to the station?"

Ted was livid. He could barely contain his anger. He swore at me as the procession began, moving at fifteen miles an hour, the policeman keeping his eye on us in the rear-view mirror.

While Ted was questioned at the desk, I was taken to a nearby office to explain what had happened.

The sergeant decided to detain Ted until he could be taken before the judge at ten o'clock to determine his mental condition, and when I went back to the waiting room, Ted had been taken down the hall to the jail. The officers suggested I go out for a walk and get some breakfast, and I did.

When I got back, I could hear his screams before I opened the door. At first I thought it was someone else—a drunk, possibly, picked up the night before. And then, as I walked back in the station, his voice ripped through me as though it were a physical thing that reached out and attacked me as I entered.

Have you ever heard a man scream? Not a yell or a bellow, not sobbing or blubbering, but a scream of fright, in which the normally deep voice breaks out of its register in a crescendo of terror, only to be repeated, with new undulations of urgency, cutting off like a gasp at the end so that you stop breathing just to hear it?

Ted was banging something metal against the bars of his

cell, or perhaps he was clanking the door itself.

"He's a real live one, all right," one policeman smiled to another.

"What's the matter?" I asked the desk sergeant quickly, and immediately Ted began yelling my name.

"Phyllis! Help me! Phyllis! Phyllis!"

"He's okay, Ma'am," the sergeant said. "Nobody's hurting him or anything."

"He sounds terrified," I said. "Did you explain to him that this is only till ten o'clock?"

"We tried to, but he just don't listen to nobody."

"Could I see him for just a moment? Tell him it's okay?"

"Sorry. Women aren't allowed back there. He'll get tired of it after a while."

They were wrong.

"Phyllis! Help! Help me! Get me out! Phyllis!" His voice trembled in panic. The banging grew louder. Ten minutes . . . fifteen . . .

"Aw, shut up," another prisoner barked at him, his sharp voice carrying down the hall. "Can it, will you?"

"Ted," I called, "I'm here. You're going to be all right."

The officer frowned. Ted was quiet for two or three minutes, then began again. I went outside and sat on the steps to get away. The noise was getting on everyone's nerves.

A patrolman came out and lit a cigarette. "How long's he been like this?"

"He's been sick for two years, but I've never heard him scream like this. He's so frightened."

"Boy, you've sure got your hands full," the officer said sympathetically. "My old lady would have left me long before this."

At nine-fifty, Ted was released. He had become so upset that he had vomited, and he looked half wild with terror.

We walked the block to the courthouse, accompanied by a policeman, and Ted was the first one on the agenda.

The judge was a man in his late fifties, genial, hearty— a large-boned man with an understanding, fatherly voice, and the aura of a benevolent monarch. He saw each of us separately, then together.

"Ted," he said, as fathers speak to naughty children, "you've been causing a lot of trouble for your wife and other people. There's a hospital in Maryland that will take you in a few weeks, and you're going to get a chance that most people don't get. Do you understand that? Can you understand that people are concerned about you?"

Ted nodded. His fear was rapidly easing. He even smiled.

"I think you should be glad your wife found you before you did something irreversible. I want you to go back to Minnesota now, and wait for that hospital in Maryland to take you. If you'll agree to go back with your wife, I'll let you leave La Crosse."

Ted agreed, bleating out his gratitude. My heart sank. I knew we would never make it. Somehow I had thought they would escort him back in a locked van.

"I don't think he'll go," I said numbly.

"Of course he'll go," the judge said, frowning at me for my negative thinking. He put an arm around both of us and walked us to the door. "Ted says he'll go and I trust him. Good luck to you both."

I could tell he was more than anxious to get us out of La Crosse and into Minnesota where we would be another state's problem. A few minutes' driving time . . .

We walked to the car unaccompanied without speaking. In the time it took to walk one block, however, Ted changed his mind. He would not go. He was tired of being a burden to me. He wanted to go off somewhere and die quietly, he said, like elephants do when they are old and useless.

I realized suddenly that I had his keys. The officers had taken everything out of his pockets and given them to me.

"Give me my wallet," Ted said, realizing it too.

"I can't," I answered.

He insisted, grabbing my arm and squeezing it hard. I told him that if he wanted to go off where I couldn't find him, he would not have been sitting on the courthouse steps where the sheriff could. I said I believed he really wanted help but was too afraid to make the decision himself. Therefore, as his wife, I would have to do it for him.

No, he said. He wouldn't go. The bloody sleeping pills hadn't worked (yes, he had taken the whole bottle), and he'd have to try something else.

I went back to see the judge, who dispatched an officer to bring Ted in a second time.

This time the monarch was less benevolent. He was already behind schedule from seeing Ted at all.

"I have two choices, Ted," he said frankly. "I will either deem you mentally incompetent and commit you to a hospital here in Wisconsin, or you will have to return with your wife and enter a hospital there. Which will it be?"

"Minnesota," Ted said grudgingly, biding his time.

"Do you have any relatives, any friends at all up there?" the judge asked me.

"An uncle and aunt," I said.

"Ask them to come down here and drive you back. See that Ted goes directly to a hospital until it's time to go East."

Those words again. Was there a passport, maybe? Or a secret word that opened the doors of a hospital and let us in? Ted became a sphinx again. He sat immobile in the judge's chambers, daring us, it seemed, to move him.

I called my poor aunt, the one unfortunate enough to have married the man who later robbed my uncles. Now she was married to someone else, trying to make a new life, and here I was dumping another loony in her lap. But she was gracious because she understood. Yes, she said, they'd come.

Why is it that people adopt a certain cheerfulness when coming face-to-face with the deranged? My aunt's smile seemed to have been chiseled into place before they reached the courthouse, and for the life of her she couldn't stop it. *We're really nice people,* the smile seemed to say, *and I know you don't want to hurt us, Ted, so don't take one step forward or I'll scream.*

It was all right. If I had been in her place, I would have felt terrified too.

"Well!" she said. "Shall we go? It's a beautiful day for a drive, isn't it?"

It was a beautiful day for a suicide, for a mass murder. When we got back to the car, Ted said he would go only on the condition that he himself drive it. If he were going into another hospital, he would go in of and by himself. He would not have somebody else driving the car. My aunt turned helplessly to me.

I realized that Ted needed to feel that he still had some control over his life. His car—the first he had ever owned—had meaning as a symbol of independence and masculinity. To sit passively by while someone else drove was the ultimate degradation. I decided to barter. I told him that he could drive providing he go straight to the veteran's hospital when we got there. He said he would go.

Thus began the 143-mile trip back, on a winding road on the bluffs overlooking the Mississippi. Ted said nothing at all the entire trip. And there was nothing much to say, because he hardly knew my relatives at all, nor they him. He sat tensely in the driver's seat, hands gripping the wheel so tightly that his knuckles showed up sharp and white, his lips moving in a silent monologue to himself. My aunt sat in the back seat, huddled against her husband, who had a nervous way of clearing his throat whenever Ted careened around a curve. I mentally practiced what I would do should Ted suddenly turn the wheel toward the river, knowing all the while that whatever I did would be too late.

On one level, I was so tired I didn't really care. I still had not even thought of a life without Ted. I had not really separated my individuality from his, could not see myself as worth much apart from him, though God knows what I was worth to anybody with Ted in tow. I found my mind wandering again, thinking of sleep, wondering idly if we might come across Mr. Moreno in his beige summer suit hitchhiking back to his hotel, and whether Ted would pick him up if we did.

On another level, however, I knew I had no right to involve my aunt in the mess—to ask her to give her life, if it came to that, should Ted decide to go over the edge.

For several years, ours had been a "taking" existence. Together Ted and I had done almost nothing for anyone else. We had called the long-suffering Dr. Pollard at odd hours. We had called upon ministers to come to our apartment. We had asked financial assistance from Ted's father and my uncles; we had given nothing to anyone in return. And now I was subjecting two more people to a reckless drive that might end with us all in the river. I was overcome with remorse. I wondered, when we stopped at a gas station, if perhaps we should tie Ted down and drive him to the hospital ourselves. But he stood at the car door waiting for us to get back in, steely-eyed with clenched jaw, and I hadn't the nerve.

We did not go off a cliff. Ted drove straight to the VA hospital and sat in the waiting room while I talked to the admitting physician. This time I knew what to say.

"My husband is suicidal, and is a danger to other people

132

as well," I said. "He once bought a gun, and struck an elderly woman with his car. I can no longer be responsible for him."

Ted was admitted immediately. The magic words: suicide, gun, injury to others.

The admission to the Sanitarium was getting closer. It was the last great hope, the ultimate test. There was nowhere to go after that. The burden on Ted must have been tremendous.

SIX

TED'S TRANSFER to the Sanitarium was only a week away and I panicked at the thought of a last minute slip-up. I phoned Dr. Pollard one final time. I told him what our monthly bill would be and Ted's reaction to it. I told him how negative Ted was feeling toward me, his father, the world in general. . . . Was it worth it, I guess I was asking. If a patient feels so hopeless, is there any sense at all in doing it?

Sometimes, Dr. Pollard said, a skilled analyst can break through that wall of fear and apathy and bring about really amazing results. As usual, I did not hear the "sometimes." I was reassured. Once I had done this for Ted, no one could accuse me of not trying.

There would be no Mr. Moreno to accompany us this time. He had written grudgingly from Albuquerque to say that he would still pay part of Ted's hospitalization if I could get him to Maryland, but that he would not be a party to moving him there, and I can't say that I blamed him. I sought the help of my perpetual friend, Charles Sweet, who—with his own brand of friendly persuasion—got Ted out to the airport and stayed with us till we passed the gate.

The walk to the plane looked like a hundred years of eternity. Ted was nervous and frightened, like a horse at the starting gate. He jumped at the slightest noise, searched every face, and moaned softly to himself as though wrestling with a decision to stay or make a run for it. I pictured him racing across the field against the shouts of the mechanics and into the propeller of an arriving plane. Such fantasies were becoming increasingly frequent. I imagined him driving off cliffs, jumping out of windows, throwing himself in the path of a truck, or hanging himself with a belt. My own rebellion against this prolonged ordeal was climaxing in a deep wish to have it ended, and my guilt at times overwhelmed me. How selfish could I be? How could I think of myself when Ted was suffering so horribly? This was the man I had promised to love, for better or worse, and now I was being put to the test. Where was my compassion, my imagination, even? Couldn't I at least guess what it must be like to feel one's sanity slipping away and be helpless to stop it?

Despite both my wish and my fears, Ted did not bolt. Inside the plane, however, he insisted on sitting by the aisle, and refused to fasten his seat belt. My panic returned. He would wait till the last minute and then make a dash for the door. The plane would rise into the air and I would be on my way to Maryland in his place. Very sneaky. I was becoming paranoid too through osmosis.

"Would you fasten your seat belt, sir?" the small stewardess asked, smiling. And when Ted hesitated, she assumed he was either deaf or didn't know how, so she did it for him.

I looked out the window and saw Charles Sweet still standing at the gate. Then the engines started and the steps were wheeled away. We were in. He couldn't get out. The first hurdle was over. Two more to go.

"Well, this is it," Ted said, feeling it too, and began the nail biting which I had noticed recently—a compulsive chewing and gnawing, oblivious to the stares of others. Every so often he would stop biting and crack his knuckles instead, and then the ritual was repeated.

He would not touch the lunch which the stewardess brought him. He was uneasy about the knobs and buttons on the arms of his seat, as though pressing the wrong one would send an electric current through him. He couldn't seem to sit still at all, and finally got up and locked himself in the rest room.

How many other women, I wondered, panicked at the thought of their husband alone in a lavatory? I realized that this was the one place he could escape us. Was he wearing a belt? Yes, I was sure of it. If he couldn't hang himself from a ceiling fixture, could he die simply by pulling it as tightly as possible about his neck and leaving it there? Would others try the door and, finding it locked, finally call the stewardess? Would she open it with her special key to find a body propped against the sink, its eyes bulging?

As the time extended into ten minutes, fifteen, and finally twenty, I watched the bottom of the door for the trickle of blood that would tell me the long wait was over. Finally, however, Ted emerged and began pacing restlessly up and down the aisle. He did not sit again till the stewardess decided he was in the way and asked him to return to his seat.

When we reached Washington, I had my plans all ready. I would move rapidly, determinedly, and give Ted no hint of ambivalence. Holding his arm, I went quickly to the baggage pickup where I instructed a redcap to hail a cab. We were swept along by the stream of passengers, and soon found ourselves seated in the back of a taxi, heading for Maryland. I never dreamed it would be so easy. One more hurdle to go—getting him through the door.

It was as though the tension were slowly oozing out of my pores. My fingers and toes seemed to go numb. I began to feel as one does after a hard day of physical work, sinking deliciously down on a soft bed. I even experienced warmth and passion by the touch of Ted's knee against mine. He would soon be someone else's problem, someone else's responsibility, and I loved him for it.

"Where 'bout in Rushville you folks going?" the driver asked.

"Five hundred East Macy Drive," I told him.

"Private home or apartment?"

I hesitated. I couldn't think of an answer. How could I call it a hospital when it looked like a house? But how on earth could I call it a private home?

"It's a . . . an institution," I said, and regretted it instantly.

There is something about the word "institution" that causes fear in the stoutest heart of even the most burly cab driver. The word, I realized, caused fear in myself. "Institution" conjures up the smell of overcooked food, antiseptics, and urine. It conjures up the sounds of dishes clattering and old people moaning and bedpans rattling on a cart down the hall. It evokes deranged people staring at their elbows and fat attendants jostling and calling to each other in the hallways. It was not my imagination that the word affected the driver. I could see his eyes in the rearview mirror, zigzagging back and forth between Ted and me.

Then I heard Ted say, "We're just visiting. We're not going to stay."

137

The driver relaxed while my own muscles went into spasm.

We had two suitcases between us; the rest would be shipped later. The cab moved slowly up East Macy Drive, searching for numbers—past the big Victorian houses with their wide porches and well-tended lawns, past the funeral parlor and through the rows of tall elms on either side of the street until we came to the wooded entrance of the Sanitarium, marked only by a small sign, "500 East Macy." Nirvana. Up the drive and into the circular turnaround.

"I'm not staying here," Ted murmured flatly, and made no move to get out. The driver paused, his hands on the baggage, and looked at us. He made no sound at all. I wondered if he were breathing.

"Don't give up now," I said to Ted.

The driver's eyes moved from me to Ted.

"All right, but I'm entering voluntarily," Ted said. "They can't keep me here. If I don't like it, I can leave. I won't be committed."

The driver took our bags inside, left them by the door, and disappeared.

We were immediately met by an administrative doctor and a social worker—pleasant, friendly faces who welcomed Ted as though he were a guest in their home. I filled out some papers while the doctor spoke with Ted, explaining the daily schedule. He would be staying in Overlook, one of the most coveted residences on the grounds because these patients had considerable freedom. I was pleased. How could Ted not like this place, these people?

Maryland, in June, was truly beautiful. The road to Overlook wound around behind the main mansion through a big open field on the hospital grounds. Having entered the Sanitarium from a shady residential street, we now found ourselves suddenly in open country, ninety acres in all, with

138

an apple orchard on one side and a big expanse of sky overhead.

We were met at Overlook by a nurse who welcomed us again, and led us to Ted's room. It was an attractive room —comfortable, with bright colors—and decorated with personal touches by the roommate who was, we discovered, being discharged in a week. Bill Goldberg was standing by the bureau when we came in, packing some things from the dresser drawers. Handsome in a mild sort of way, quiet, but with a spark of humor, he greeted Ted cordially, explaining that he would be leaving soon and offering to show Ted around in the short time he had left. I liked him instantly. If, when Bill came here, he was as sick as Ted, then this was indeed a place of miracles.

Overlook, in fact, looked like a retreat for artists and writers—clean, attractive, like someone's country home. People moved in and out the door with tennis rackets or sat in the big living room reading and listening to music. We sat down too, the nurse, Ted, and I, and talked about where we would go from here. I would be staying in a private home nearby till I found an apartment within walking distance of the Sanitarium. I could come to visit every afternoon if I liked, evenings also. Ted remained mute, never taking his eyes off me, like a small child on the first day of nursery school.

Well, I said, I had a lot to do, so would unpack and come back the following day. I leaned over to kiss Ted as I stood up.

He clutched my hand in a death grip and it was then I noticed that his face was contorted by fear and I felt him tremble.

"I don't want to stay here," Ted said resolutely, standing up too. "I'm going with you."

"You can't do that, Ted," I explained. "The treatment requires that you be an inpatient for a while. Later you can live with me."

Ted edged toward the screen door, ignoring the gentle voice of the nurse. His teeth were chattering and he looked sick to his stomach, as though he might vomit.

"Honey, you're going to be all right here," I said. "They won't let anything happen to you. It'll be okay. I'll see you tomorrow. Please trust me."

Ted took my arm and turned me away so that the nurse couldn't hear. "They'll kill me here," he whispered. "I've seen the signs. They hate me. The other patients—that one over there . . ."

I neared the screen and found a tall male aide waiting with his hand on the knob, holding it open for me. I had been told that, if necessary, three doctors from the Sanitarium would certify Ted mentally ill in order to keep him there legally.

"Phyllis!" Ted said as I stepped outside and the aide locked the screen after me.

"Ted, let's sit down together and talk," the aide said. "I know it seems strange at first, but . . ."

"Phyllis!" Ted called, his panic rising, pushing hard against the locked screen. "I'm not staying here. They can't do this! I wasn't committed."

"Ted, you have to have help," I said. "I'll see you tomorrow. I promise."

He looked as he had looked standing at the window of the train on his way to Albuquerque. He looked as he had when I woke up in the middle of the night and found his face within inches of mine, eyes wide, staring. . . . And as I walked quickly down the steps, he sounded as he'd sounded that one morning in the jail at La Crosse.

"Phyllis!" he pleaded, pressing his face against the screen,

140

straining to see me as I went down the walk. "Phyllis! Phyllis!"

I could hear him all the way down the road, and when the pleading stopped, and I turned to look, he was still standing there, staring after me like a deserted waif.

I did not stop walking till I was around the bend. Then I sat down in the grass in the open field and cried with sadness and relief.

I spent the first few nights in Rushville in a bedroom of a huge private home a few blocks from the Sanitarium, owned by a gracious, genteel woman who often provided guest rooms for relatives of patients. She left me completely alone.

It was nine before I awoke the next day, and I was surprised by a chorus of birdcalls, as though I had bedded down in a tropical forest. I did not know that so many varieties of birds existed—chirps and trills and timorous little purrings that one never hears on the cold streets of big cities. And, through the open window, the faint fragrance of honeysuckle.

How many other wives or husbands had spent their first few nights in this room, exhausted from the ordeal of admitting a relative to the Sanitarium? How many mothers and fathers? How much more painful it must be to leave a son or daughter, how profound the remorse and guilt, justified or not. I wondered if there were birds around Overlook, and if Ted had heard them too.

It seemed right that the Sanitarium should be in Maryland, for Maryland and madness, or at least the abnormal, were linked indelibly in my mind. As a young girl, I used to come to Maryland to visit my father's parents, perhaps once every four years. They lived in a small town south of Marlboro where my grandfather was pastor of the community

141

church, and his wife, the practical nurse and midwife, took live-in patients that no one else wanted. The state paid my grandmother a small stipend for taking care of them, and they became devoted servants, ever mindful that if it weren't for my grandmother, they would be wards in a state hospital.

I used to wonder, privately, which was worse. When my grandmother seated herself in the glider beneath the big beech tree and told Lou and Albert to bring her this or that, I wondered if it really were the best arrangement. But here, at least, they had freedom, responsibilities, and praise when they'd earned it, and they responded with an outpouring of loyalty to my grandparents.

Lou was a small wiry-looking woman with a pointed chin, who wore her hair pulled back in a tight bun. She suffered epileptic seizures and stuttered severely. It was rumored darkly that before Mammaw (my grandmother) took her in, she had "run around with men" and had borne a daughter out of wedlock. In all the months I spent during summers at my grandparents' home, I never actually saw Lou have a seizure. But several times I heard a thud and saw my grandmother rush into an adjoining room to hold Lou's tongue down with a spoon.

As a young girl, I sought desperately to view Lou with concern, and took my turn sitting in the kitchen while she prepared dinner to make sure she didn't have a seizure and cut herself with a knife. She would tell me stories about the birth of a calf or how the bull got loose in the garden, and we considered ourselves fast friends.

At the same time, I struggled with the suspicion that my interest in Lou was more curiosity than compassion. I heard stories of her having seizures in church, halfway through my grandfather's sermon, and wetting the pew, or having a seizure by the stove and scalding herself with hot water, and I was both terrified and awed. In the most unusual episode of all, someone told me that Lou had been sent to the crawl space in the attic to search for something for my grandmother, who was sick in bed at the time, had had a seizure, fallen through the plaster, and landed on top of Mammaw in the bed below. Though I tried valiantly to keep a straight face when we retold this story, and though I never once saw anyone laugh at poor Lou's misfortunes, the thought of her coming down through the ceiling on top of Mammaw seemed hilarious to me. It required the greatest self-control to hold the laughter in. What on earth was the matter with me? My grandfather could well have preached an entire sermon on the demons in me alone.

Then there was Albert, a young man when he came to Mammaw's, mentally retarded, who was the object of taunts and abuse from neighborhood children, and who, despite his handicap, often showed more maturity than they. Whereas Lou stuttered fiercely, her eyes blinking as she struggled to get out the words, Albert's drawl was painfully slow and his words were slurred, as though his mouth was full of oatmeal. He had large ears that stuck straight out from the sides of his head, looking for all the world like Alfred E. Neuman on the cover of *Mad* magazine. But he was an extremely hard worker, doing all the outside chores, the planting and hoeing, mowing and raking, feeding of the animals, mending fences, and whatever else needed to be done. When he went to the post office once to get the mail, a group of boys followed, chanting that Albert was dumb and didn't know anything. "I know enough to keep my mouth shut," he had replied, and Mammaw praised him for his answer and repeated this story many times to company while Albert stood by and beamed.

In fact, Mammaw was the caretaker not only of Lou and Albert's bodies, but their souls as well. She insisted on daily devotions read aloud in her bedroom, and set herself the task of teaching poor Albert to read. When he often gave up in despair, she reminded him that Hell awaited those who didn't try, the same thing she had told him when she found him masturbating and insisted he stop. And so he laboriously memorized a few verses, and it was enough to satisfy her.

The third patient, a Mr. Wells, was kept indoors in a special room beyond the dining room, and it was Mr. Wells I feared above all else. I cannot say why, because he was completely bedridden and never said a word. But he had fierce eyes beneath a monstrous set of brows, and his behavior was so bizarre that it terrified me. Once, when everyone else was busy, I was asked to carry his dinner tray to him and to sit and wait while he ate it to make sure he didn't choke. I begged for another job, pleaded, but was told that others had taken their turn at it and it was now mine.

Mr. Wells must have been in his eighties. He was absolutely senile, but his body looked well and strong. Not only that, but he refused to wear clothes, and it was all we could do to keep him covered with a bed sheet. On this particular day, as I entered his room with the tray, my heart thumping, I found him sitting upright, propped up in his hospital bed, eagerly awaiting his food, his one remaining pleasure. I set the tray on his lap and quickly retreated to a chair in the far corner.

He did not take his eyes off me once. His face always wore a deep intense scowl and his eyes were huge, like a man on the verge of rage. He made no sound, spoke no words, but ran his hand over the tray until his fingers grasped something, and then he ate, pieces of food falling down on the sheet, while he continued his ferocious stare.

I could not bear it. I cringed, I looked away, I picked up a book and pretended to read, but whenever I looked up, there were those eyes—the eyes of madness—staring into me.

He picked up an ear of buttered corn and proceeded to rip off the kernels with his teeth, some falling onto his bare chest where they stuck like warts. And suddenly, he stuffed one end of the cob itself into his mouth, took a bite, and began chewing.

That did it. I rushed from the room screaming that Mr. Wells was eating the cob, upsetting Lou who went out onto the porch and had a seizure. I was never asked to attend the old man again and I was never sorry. . . . Now, as I looked out the window at the purple clay soil of a bank at the back of the yard, I remembered the purple soil of my grandfather's farm and the madness I had encountered there, and felt I was home again.

There was only one apartment complex within walking distance of the Sanitarium. It was in a rundown area about a mile away, but the rent was low. So I leased one of the apartments, located the bus stop and drugstore where I would take my meals temporarily, bought a county paper, and then—that evening—walked back to Overlook to see Ted.

An aide met me at the door and apologized for the fact that I had walked all that way for nothing. Ted was not there, he explained, but had been transferred to the main building. He was sure that the nurse there would answer all my questions.

I walked quickly back down the winding road, through the pasture without bothering to look at any of it. Change, I felt, was the last thing Ted needed right now. He needed the security of being in one room, in one house, having one doctor . . . the feeling that he belonged, that he could count on something. Overlook had been so lovely. What had happened?

I bombarded the receptionist with questions and she referred me to one of the administrative doctors. The change had been made, he said, because they felt the third floor

145

would be more appropriate for Ted in his agitated condition. He would need to be under closer supervision.

Agitated condition?

The staff at Overlook, I was told, had planned a picnic that afternoon, and Ted, as a new resident, was of course invited. He had calmed down considerably after I had left the day before, seemed resigned to being there, and the nurse felt he might enjoy being outside with the others. They were playing a ball game in a nearby field when they discovered that Ted was missing. On checking, they found that he had slipped back to the parking lot, started a car, and then had lain down behind it with his head by the exhaust pipe. Obviously, the doctor said, he was not ready for this type of freedom yet, and would be on the third floor indefinitely. Would I like to see him?

Despite my familiarity with mental hospitals, with Ted, with the bizarre and inexplicable, I was not prepared for what I found on third. The self-operated elevator at the back of the building was in use so the aide suggested we walk up. On second, I was startled by a face at the square window of the door—a young, deranged woman looking at me through tangled strands of short, straight hair. She had a hostile, sneering, curious stare—as though it were a mere quirk of fate that she was on that side of the door and I on the other, and perhaps she was right. The stare unnerved me. I found it more difficult to accept the bizarre and hostile in women than in men. When a face that is supposed to be gentle becomes violent instead, the flesh creeps. And when the woman began banging on the door and rattling the handle, the aide said simply, "The door is locked," and we went on up to third.

We stood outside the locked door and the aide rang the buzzer. By the time the nurse opened it, we had attracted a small welcoming committee.

"This is Mrs. Moreno," the aide said, and I was in.

The deranged I had met so far were, at their most miserable worst, simply silent. The troubled young men in the veteran's hospitals sat moodily off to one side or shook their heads occasionally in wordless dialogue with themselves. Stepping onto the third floor of the Sanitarium was like entering a Goya painting.

They were all men, mostly of college age. Here were the offspring of some of America's richest families, and their sickness had reduced them to a common level with the most indigent patients in the state hospitals. Some of the families were renowned. One of the patients, in fact, had been a Rhodes scholar. Here were young men who had carried on their shoulders the highest hopes of their families. Insanity, like nakedness, reduces us all to one.

My eyes took them in one at a time, like characters in a drama. In contrast to the polite, tense voices at Overlook, there were inhuman sounds—babbles and grunts, mumbling, crying, and moaning. Others smiled to themselves, moving swiftly around, going nowhere. In one corner a man crouched with his face to the wall, his head hanging down on his chest. Another sat on a bench in the hallway, hands on his knees, rocking violently forward and back to some secret inner rhythm, smiling without seeing. A tall man stood in a doorway in a pair of loose pajamas and as we passed on the way to Ted's room, something prompted the nurse to say firmly, "Go to the bathroom, Henry," and instantly the man turned and fled into the open bath.

The third floor did not have the country-home appearance of Overlook. In place of stone fireplace and rugs, the floors were tiled, the chairs vinyl, the curtainless windows covered with heavy metal screens. We had entered into a large common room that served as living room. From there, a hallway led to the front of the mansion, and there were perhaps five bedrooms on either side. Each bedroom had a door with a small square window in it, but no lock. The communal bathroom had no door at all.

I was only twenty feet from Ted's door when suddenly a tall lean youth strode quickly toward me, one finger in the air, like a Bible Belt preacher. He came so fast I was sure he would knock me over, but he stopped only inches away.

"Who asked this woman to come into our presence?" he demanded. "By what authority does this Jezebel appear before us? She is a harlot, and shall be cast off into everlasting torment—a whore, a villainous, loathsome creature . . . the dregs of the earth, a slut. . . ."

"This is Mrs. Moreno," the nurse said quietly, as an aide moved in to help us pass. "She's come to see her husband."

The orator reached out to touch me, but the aide put an arm around his shoulder and genially led him out to the screened porch in back. The nurse opened the door to Ted's room, closed it behind me, and we were alone.

He was lying on his bed, fully dressed, staring at the ceiling, hands under his head. The bed on the other side of the room was unmade, but Ted's roommate was out.

"Hello," Ted smiled wanly.

"Hello," I said, and sat down. The room had more of the personal touch than the rest of the floor. There were pictures on the walls, some of them obviously drawn by the roommate. The bedspreads were colorful, and there were closets and dressers for clothes.

"Well, they put me up here with the loonies," Ted said. "So I see."

"It's better this way," he said. His voice was strangely meek and gentle—loving, even. "The Commies don't want me to have it so good."

He had to suffer. It was all down in the contract, the unwritten contract he kept in the back of his mind.

"Thirty-three years old," he said sadly, referring to his approaching birthday. "That was the age Christ died, you know."

"And?"

"Though I have seen my head (grown slightly bald) brought in
    upon a platter,
I am no prophet—and here's no great matter;
I have seen the moment of my greatness flicker,
And I have seen the eternal Footman hold my coat, and snicker,
And in short, I was afraid."

He was afraid, and he admitted that fear. Wasn't that a good sign, that he could talk about it? Weren't we all afraid of something, some unmentionable something that we kept deep down in our darker selves, acknowledging scarcely to anyone?

All my life I had been told by my Christian relatives what glories awaited us in heaven. When my preacher grandfather died, Mammaw turned suddenly away from his casket and said desperately to me, "Your grandfather is with the angels now," but her voice ended with a question mark, and years later, on her own deathbed, she talked fearfully of the Deep River Man who was coming to get her. Would it have been easier, I wonder, all those years, if she had said out loud that, glories or not, she was scared?

Ted was witnessing the death not of his body but of his mind. Perhaps that was the greatest terror of all.

I moved into my new apartment the following day. I purchased a cheap aluminum cot and a few dishes, and hung my clothes in the closet. I would contact the storage firm in Minnesota about delivering our household things, books, and piano, and would go to the Goodwill store nearby to purchase a few pieces of secondhand furniture and a bed.

That night, as I lay on the cot in the center of the empty

room, I wondered about myself and my life. Every hour that passed, I calculated, was costing us two dollars at the Sanitarium. Every day, forty-eight dollars, every week, three hundred and fifty dollars, and I didn't even have a job.

The shadow of the casement window frame was etched against one wall where the streetlight entered and gave the room the appearance of a cell. Was it worth it to drag a patient kicking and screaming for treatment? How could a patient get well knowing that every breath he took cost more than his family could afford? How long before my own resentment grew so strong I could not hide it?

Would it have been better for both of us if I had not gone after him in Albuquerque? Had refused to go get him in La Crosse? What about the feeling that I had driven one man mad and nobody else would want me? If we separated, if I washed my hands of him finally and just gave up—would I go on worrying about him the rest of my natural life anyway?

All the rapture that I thought I would feel *if only* the Sanitarium would accept my husband was now due. We were here, he was in, where was the jubilation? What was holding it up? I closed my eyes and tried to sleep. Ted was their problem now. They knew our funds were limited. They knew they had just so many months to get him in shape. Let them worry about it, not me. Just for tonight, anyway. At least I knew he was safe.

Something brushed against my wrist. I wriggled my hand and felt the something drop off the ends of my fingers. I got up and turned on the light. The room was alive with roaches. They were huge, with wings, and could hurl themselves at me from almost any angle. I couldn't stay there.

When morning came, I put everything I owned on the cot, bought a can of roach powder, and made a wide nine-foot circle around my cot. Then I set out on foot to look for a job and ended up in an employment office.

Question: what does an employment office and psychoanalysis have in common? Answer: each forces you to look at yourself as you really are.

Education? A junior college diploma, a year of assorted correspondence courses, and a couple of night school classes.

Length of residence in Maryland? Three days.

Personal status? Married, so to speak.

Spouse's occupation? Unemployed.

Reason for moving to Maryland? To admit said spouse to a mental institution.

Can you type? A little.

Shorthand? No.

Driver's license? No.

Foreign languages? None.

Experience? Clinical secretary, elementary school teacher (plus a short stint as a women's locker-room attendant):

Last three addresses and reasons for leaving? Oh God, do I have to list them all?

I discovered I was not really much good for anything. I couldn't teach in the county without a degree. I couldn't even substitute. I did not qualify as a secretary, accountant, nurse, beautician, or cab driver. Who would want a soft-spoken, anxiety-ridden young woman with a ten-thousand-dollar debt over her head, whose husband might, at any moment, hang himself? Who wanted an employee whose sole ability, it seemed, was writing weird little stories for magazines no one had ever heard of?

I was hired finally by the psychology office in the Board of Education to type up clinical reports. The salary was laughable, but I was desperate.

There would be no secrets, I decided, as I set out for work each morning from my little cot surrounded by the great China Wall of roach powder. In my new life, in my new town, I would not make the mistake of covering up again for Ted. And so I contracted a sort of verbal diarrhea. I told everyone before they could ask. I talked readily, answered questions willingly, and the magic of being candid made friends. Come to dinner, people said. Go to the movies with us. Stop by the house.

I found another small apartment in a private home directly across the street from the Sanitarium. Life was easing up. I could cross the street now to visit Ted each evening. I could walk to work as well as to a Unitarian church. I had made a few friends, including Bill Goldberg, Ted's former roommate at Overlook, who now had a job. They included me in their plans, made me laugh, and restored in me some sense of worth.

My time was varied. I met new people, learned new things. For Ted, however, shut up on third floor by choice, life was a cage of his own construction. Though he was taken on short trips with other patients, to movies, to the crafts shop, to socials and concerts, he made no effort to cooperate, showed no will to participate. It was too soft, he declared, too plush. Too luxurious, too kind. The Communists were angry.

And so one day in the crafts shop, he swallowed a hunk of steel wool in the hope that it would cut his intestinal tract to ribbons, and that he would bleed to death internally, saving us the job of mopping him up. It had no effect. He was becoming a collector of stomach objects.

It was important, I knew, not to become impatient with his lack of progress because of our mounting debt. He had problems enough without worrying about the financial part of it too. He was, after all, getting four hours of intensive psychotherapy a week. *Something* had to be taking root. Surely, in the long run, the patience and kindness and individual attention he received would pay off and trust would develop.

Included in a patient's fee were weekly sessions with the social worker for members of the patient's family if they wanted it. Many of the wealthy simply came to Maryland, dropped off their deranged, and left, talking to the social worker only when they came for visits.

But I needed these weekly sessions. Because of my experience at the veteran's hospital, I had entered her bright plant-laden office expecting long lists of things I must do for Ted, of ways I must change, of subjects to be avoided and topics to be emphasized. I expected to have my marriage laid out on the desk and dissected, with a map showing me just where I had made the wrong turns. I expected sermons on wifehood, with assigned readings and true-and-false tests. I expected a diploma or something when I was through, certifying me of maturity, with a signed vow that I would never again drive a man to distraction. There was none of it. The social worker was interested in me and *my* life, in *my* plans, *my* interests, *my* goals. She was not as much interested in how my mistakes may have affected Ted as how his might have affected me. She was my lifeboat. She cared. She really cared.

If I ever inherit a million dollars and crack up, let me go to the Rushville Sanitarium. There was approximately one psychoanalyst to every four patients. The aides, who were young college men, showed a remarkable capacity for empathy themselves. While state and veteran's hospitals are so understaffed that they can often give special attention only to those who are creating disturbances, the Sanitarium had orderlies and nurses and aides in profusion. If a patient was unusually depressed and withdrawn, it was not uncommon to see an aide put an arm around him and sit talking quietly for twenty minutes. They were like brothers—tender, caring relatives—whose concern and respect were evident. Truthfulness was one of the basics. Patients were not coddled or patronized, but treated with honesty. Nurses spoke softly, unhurried. The staff of occupational therapy came to the floor daily to give individual attention to the patients—organizing a party, taking someone out for a walk, going to the bank with another, or playing a game of cards. There seemed to be infinite time, infinite patience, infinite resources.

There were rules, to be sure, but they were always under review, and were bent when necessary for the good of the patient. If Ted felt too depressed to come down to the living room, yet wanted to see me, I was invited up. If he seemed unusually glad to have me there, the nurses would ask if I would like to stay for dinner with him in his room. It was as though everyone were searching continually for ways to help a patient relate, to help make things easy for the relatives as well.

At the same time, there were risks and I understood them. There was no fence or wall around the estate. When a patient was deemed ready for grounds privileges—a staff decision—he would be granted some freedom. It was possible, of course, that he might eventually hurl himself under a truck or off a bridge, but getting well, the doctors explained, meant taking some chances.

The Sanitarium itself, with its accompanying cottages, blended in nicely with the surrounding neighborhood, and was proof that an asylum for the insane could operate quite well in a residential area. I never heard wild screams. I never saw patients running around outside naked. The neighbors accepted the Sanitarium because they had learned there was nothing to fear. There were no signs at the drive to keep people out, no gates or guards. Anyone could stroll up the driveway and walk around the grounds without raising eyebrows. Only the built-in bumps in the driveway, at intervals, reminded those who drove through that there were reasons for driving with caution. So unless one knew that it was an institution, unless one knew the signs, one might guess that it was the estate of a quiet country gentleman.

The most obvious sign, to one living right across the street, was the number of fire alarms. I never knew if these calls were turned in by the patients or the staff, but it seemed that Rushville's Volunteer Fire Department rolled up the drive an excessive number of times and always left a few minutes later.

Another sign was the common sight of a patient and aide walking into town together. The aides dressed in street clothes and looked no different from anyone else. But the residents always knew. Usually it was by the disheveled appearance of the female patients, though it may have taken them an hour to dress. Or perhaps it was the peculiar gait or the droop of the shoulders or the unwillingness to look a stranger in the face. The aides usually said hello to those they passed. The patients rarely spoke. Or perhaps they spoke too much and had to be urged on.

If one did not pass patients on the street, he could tell that the Sanitarium was something out of the ordinary by the number of Cadillacs and Lincoln Continentals that arrived with visitors. And if one stood out on the sidewalk and looked through the trees, he might see a middle-aged couple trying to coax a son or daughter into their limousine to go for a Sunday drive. Or it might be an elegantly dressed woman sitting primly, self-consciously, on a bench out under the trees, painfully trying to pretend tolerance for the snickering, babbling girl with the stringy hair that was her daughter.

I felt like an interloper with respect to the Sanitarium. We

155

did not really belong, Ted and I. We did not have the limitless funds necessary to place a patient in its care and say,
"Here, for as long as it takes, is your home. No one will
hurry you. Take all the time you need." I could have lived
for two weeks on what it was costing to support Ted for one
day. The doctors knew this. They had cautioned me about
the expense. They had suggested it was far more than we
could afford. But I had begged. Oh, how I had begged. And
they were willing to take a chance because I wanted it so
badly and because Ted was, after all, quite reachable on
occasion.

What the wealthy took for granted was an agonizing decision for me, despite the loan from my uncles. What was
mere change in their pocket was a week's wages in mine.
The first time the nurse asked if I would like to stay and
eat dinner with Ted in his room, I was delighted with the
courtesy, with the chance to be together, only to be dismayed
at the end of the month when I discovered that the cost of
my dinner had been added to the bill.

Ted's condition vacillated between seeming progress and
reversals. At times he declared that the doctor was, perhaps,
his friend after all—at other times, the enemy. There were
days he craved my presence, greeted me passionately, hugging
me to him as though he would never let me go. Other times
he lay stiffly on his bed, refusing even to look me in the
face. Some weeks the social worker would report that Ted's
doctors were pleased with his progress, that he was voluntarily socializing with the other patients, and my heart would
leap at the news, devouring more than was really there,
telling myself that maybe this was the breakthrough and
that Ted would be OK. And then I would hear the following week that Ted had been withdrawn for several days and
was talking again of suicide. Slowly I became less elated and

156

more cautious upon hearing good news. I would wait and see.

One day in autumn I had run the gauntlet of patients on third, passed the young man rocking on the bench and the preacher in the hallway, and made it to Ted's room to find him warm, communicative, and frankly sexual. He hugged me tenderly, pressing himself against me, and edged me over to the bed where we lay down, embracing.

I was delighted with this change in him and all my old feelings about him came flowing through. It was as though his flesh were warm again for the first time, as though our skins were in tune. I knew we couldn't make love there in full view of anyone who might look through the little square window, but I gave in to his kisses and caresses. It was as though Ted had come home—the hands, the body, the scents, the whispers. . . .

There was a shout in the hall outside. We looked up to see the preacher, glaring at us through the window, his face contorted with indignation, his voice agitated.

"Thou shalt not commit adultery!" he bellowed excitedly. "There is an adulteress on this floor! Here she is—a woman of death!" He began banging on the door. "A vile corrupt harlot of stinking flesh and oily limbs! Out with this corruption! Out with this abomination! Cast her away!"

I felt as I had felt once on the farm with my second set of grandparents—farmers of German descent—when I had been caught trying to look up "sodomy" in the dictionary. It was during one of my summer visits when it was discovered that the beloved male choir director of the small rural church had been corrupting the morals of the young, and the weekly county newspaper carried the word "sodomy" in the headlines. All my relatives went whispering about in shocked voices but would not tell me what the choir director had done, and when I tried to look up the word myself, the dictionary was yanked from my hands and placed on a high shelf.

Here, however, I was the accused, and my crime was rapidly attracting the attention of everyone on third floor.

The bellowing stopped as abruptly as it had started. A nurse's face appeared briefly at the window and then disappeared. The preacher was led away. Ted lay back down beside me, caressing my arms.

"Oh, god, I wish I was out of here and we were in our own bed," he murmured.

"I want it too, Ted. It's been a long time. . . ."

On Friday, the social worker told me that if I liked, Ted could come over for short visits on weekends, that the hospital staff had held a consultation and decided it might be a good idea, good for Ted. I knew that the staff had decided that if they didn't want semen on their bedspreads and hysteria in the hall, they'd better give Ted and me a place that was really private. Besides, it was a good sign, an encouraging one, and I was delighted to have Ted come to the apartment. The circumstances, however, were a little complex.

On Saturdays, if Ted were in the mood, an aide would escort him across the street and sit downstairs on the front porch for an hour or two reading *The New Yorker* while Ted and I made love upstairs. Sometimes the landlady came out and talked with the aide to the accompaniment of the squeaks and thumps of our ancient bed. And finally, when we had talked and kissed and possibly slept a little, the aide would knock politely on the door and ask if Mr. Moreno cared to go back now. Mr. Moreno never cared to go back, but he went.

What if I screamed, I always wondered. What if the aide mistook a cry of passion for a call for help? What if he ran

158

upstairs to find the door locked and the landlady, in panic, called the police? Would they crawl up on the roof and come crashing through the window? Would they break down the French doors that separated my two rooms from the rest of the upstairs? Or would the Rushville Fire Department make one of its trial runs and use the hook and ladder?

There was something about having sex under such extraordinary circumstances that gave our afternoon lovemaking an air of unreality—ludicrous, yet necessary. How much was the aide earning, sitting down below waiting for that final spasm to pass between us? What other hospitals could afford enough aides to permit such luxuries to the patients? And yet, how important it was, and how sad that the privilege was so exclusive.

In September, I applied for a high-paying job as assistant executive secretary for a local education association. The advertisement stressed that the primary job of the assistant was to edit a monthly newsletter for teachers. The social worker at the Sanitarium saw it first and suggested I might like to apply.

I did not think I could qualify. By no stretch of the imagination could I call myself an editor or an executive secretary. But the salary would be a big help in paying for Ted's mounting expenses, so I applied. To my astonishment, I was hired, though I discovered later that there had been considerable discussion over whether my husband was in a bona fide mental institution or one for the treatment of alcoholism by a similar name. Only when I assured them that Ted was truly psychotic, the genuine article, was my appointment made official. Chalk one up for schizophrenia.

Immediately, I was enmeshed in county politics, board-of-education sessions, public hearings, and night meetings. It was imperative that I learn to drive. I bought a secondhand

Chevy for six hundred dollars, persuaded a friend to teach me to drive, and got a license. I felt like a bird. I could go anywhere I liked, depended on no one. Someone had opened the door of my cage. Then I discovered that the insurance company which had insured Ted would not insure me. Guilt by association. I had to try elsewhere.

Ted, however, did not welcome these changes. He was not part of them, and it made him even more anxious. He had no real contact with the outside world except for occasional trips to town with the other patients and his weekend visits to my apartment. He felt that life was passing him by and became obsessed with Mozart's *Requiem*. Over and over again he played it, maintaining that it had been written not only as a prelude to Mozart's death, but to his own.

Then there was the OP, or Orgasm Phenomenon. I discovered that for the first two minutes or so after orgasm, Ted was suddenly sane and rational. For at least one hundred and twenty seconds, he would lie limp and relaxed beside me, as though awakening from a dream, expressing surprise at his illness, surprise that he hadn't seen the senselessness of his delusions, appalled at his paranoia, hopeful for the future, and appreciative of his doctors.

"I *am* sick!" he would declare in astonishment, and pull me close to him. "How could I have thought these things? Where did I get these ideas? It's been my imagination all along! You know, I think I *will* get well!"

And I, as though welcoming him back from a three-year trip, would stroke and caress him and assure him that he was indeed on the way to recovery.

But as his relaxed body lay resting, the tensions which had been swept away came creeping back. His muscles locked, his arms grew rigid, and soon, his shaky voice would whisper again, "It's all a trick to make me think they've forgotten about me, isn't it? But they haven't."

Did you ever consider the orgasm as the ultimate shock treatment, Dr. Pollard? Has anyone ever done a study? Is there a way to harness sexual energy—a pill, perhaps—that would keep a patient in a perpetual state of post-orgasmic euphoria? The side effects are all pleasant—no broken ribs or loss of memory. . . .

My life became divided between my new job and Ted, and being married to him did not make my work easy. Our anniversary happened to fall during the first week of my employment, and I was startled to look up from my desk that morning to see Ted, accompanied by an aide, striding toward me with a dozen red roses. He remembered. He cared. It was a good sign, wasn't it? As the office personnel gaped, I introduced him, showed him around, and delivered him once more to the bodyguard waiting at the door.

In mid-October, Mr. Moreno arrived for an unexpected visit and announced that he was canceling all further support for Ted's treatment. He could see no improvement in his son, he said, and had been getting very little information by letter. Why should he pay out any more of his hard-earned money to a hospital that wouldn't even tell him what he wanted to know? Why did he have to fly all the way out from Albuquerque?

The staff scheduled a conference, including Mr. Moreno, Ted's administrative doctor, the social worker, and myself. Ted's father sat on one side of the conference room in his off-white suit and string tie like a miniature Colonel Sanders with an Italian accent. He fired off questions in rapid succession, for which there were no answers, and went on to the next one without waiting for a reply, even when there were. How much longer would Ted be here? Why wasn't

161

he getting any better? What was there to show for all the money he had paid out so far? What guarantee was there that once Ted got well he would even be speaking to the father who had paid half the bill?

And then he turned on me. What was the real reason I had spirited his son away to Maryland instead of Rochester? Why hadn't I coaxed Ted to write to his parents more often? Why hadn't I given them more information myself? As his anger increased, he began to sputter; he had read my letters to Ted before we were married, he confessed without one iota of shame, and was convinced that I had lured Ted into marriage. It was I and that evil psychiatrist who had turned Ted from a peace-loving man of God into an atheist who no longer respected his parents. What's more, he declared, warming to the sound of his own voice, he himself had recently hired a retired FBI agent to drive him around the University to investigate the place firsthand, and he had come to the inescapable conclusion that Communists were indeed in control, just as Ted had said. What his son needed now was to get out in New Mexico's fresh air and sunshine, away from both me and his books, where he would thrive on the word of God and his mother's home cooking.

I knew I was in the company of experts and did not have to handle this one. But the thought of Mr. M. in his wide-brimmed hat, investigating the University, was enough to boggle the mind. Did he even get out of the car, do you imagine? I cannot describe the relief of being in the presence of paranoia and not having to respond to it.

The doctors quietly explained that Mr. M. was a free agent, and that he had the right to withdraw his support if he indeed felt that to be best. But they explained that whatever had happened in the past, Ted was here now, that he had made some progress, though not a lot, and that to withdraw financial support now would be to punish and confuse him still further. There were, unfortunately, no answers to most of his questions. No one could force Ted to write to his parents, and no one could really estimate how long the treatment might have to continue. They were aware of our financial situation and would put him on outpatient status just as soon as they possibly could. But it was unfair to Ted to uproot him again. After all, he had been hospitalized once in New Mexico and it hadn't worked out. . . .

The upshot was that Mr. M. thought better of it after he had calmed down, grudgingly reconsidered, and said he would pay for six more months, but that was it.

Outside on the steps, before he got in the taxi, he turned to me.

"Phyllis," he said. "I don't want to be enemies with you."

"I don't want to be enemies either, Dad Moreno," I said earnestly. "We both love Ted. We both want him to get well. It's been hard on you, too."

He started to say more and then stopped. If we delved any deeper we would soon reach disagreements which would negate the truce. And so we said good-bye.

His visit did not affect Ted at all, one way or the other. There were too many other things to worry about, and he felt that his execution date was getting closer.

My job was becoming more difficult. What my boss had failed to stress in the interview was that I would be a substitute for him on occasion—that I would be expected to carry out the managerial responsibilities of our association in the various schools, give speeches and politick as required.

I knew little about management, less about political manipulations, and embarrassed my startled boss at a school board hearing by naïvely applauding a speaker who opposed almost everything our organization stood for. Perhaps he thought he could train me and I thought I could learn, because I doggedly stuck it out, attending all the meetings with photographers and reporters from the county paper who were becoming my closest circle of friends.

After work each day, I came home to play the piano, sometimes for an hour or two. I scarcely heard the music, going much too fast, playing too loud—a ritualistic exercise, devoid of depth or expression or soul—a physical plunking of the keys, a therapeutic release which left my arms limp, my shoulders relaxed, and drowned out all the remembered sounds and voices of the third floor across the street.

I lived for *Time* magazine, the *Washington Post,* and Edward P. Morgan's newscasts. I gulped down the national and international news, the gossip about people, the trials of Algeria, famines, earthquakes, troubles of every sort. Welcome to the human race, they seemed to say. You are not alone. I found it strangely comforting. I learned to appreciate instant pleasures by saying to myself, "Yes, there are all sorts of things to deal with later, but right now the bed is warm or the water is cool or this apple is delicious."

I was invited out almost every holiday, but I made it a point to spend half of it with Ted at the Sanitarium. I went back to Oakton for a few days after Christmas, to a friend's home on Thanksgiving, and Bill Goldberg took me to a party on New Year's Eve as a brother might escort his sister to a fraternity dance. On several occasions I tried to include Ted in my social life. I took him to church, and once to a party, but his agonized indecision as to whether or not he should go kept him upset till the last minute, and we always arrived late. Then he was miserable all evening. It seemed kinder, somehow, not to put this burden on him just yet.

In early January, I decided to give a dinner party myself in appreciation for all those friends who had been so kind to me—a huge spaghetti feast followed by piano, ragtime, songs—a sort of family reunion of friends. We had just eaten and were gathering around the piano when a call came from the Sanitarium. Ted was missing, a troubled nurse reported. Could he possibly be with me?

SEVEN

THERE HAD BEEN an unusually heavy snowfall the day before.

"How long has he been gone?" I asked.

She wasn't sure. Someone thought they had seen him in his room two hours ago.

Had he taken his overcoat?

No.

What should I do?

Stay home in case he tries to reach you, she told me. They were contacting the police.

There were ninety acres of hospital grounds to hide in, and all of Rushville as well. How many times need a person try suicide before he succeeds?

I wanted it over with, I knew—resolved. Was this what life would be like for me—a desperate struggle to keep a man alive who was just as desperate to destroy himself? And what was so unique about that? Wives of drug addicts and alcoholics faced this every day. Heart patients and diabetics who did not watch their diets put a similar strain on their families. Other wives learned to live with it, to adjust. But was it worth it? Was it worth the emotional upheaval, the screaming down in the gut, the heart palpitations, the sacrifice of my own stability to keep a man alive who preferred it otherwise?

The party broke up. People asked if there was anything they could do. No, nothing. One of the men, in what he probably felt was a gesture of comfort, offered to spend the night. No, thank you. The last thing in the world I needed was another complication.

Ted had been gone long enough to commit suicide by now. He had been gone long enough to cover his body with snow and freeze to death. It was long enough to get out on a highway and hurl himself in front of a passing truck, to cut his femoral artery and bleed to death. I waited, ashamed of my fantasies.

At one in the morning, the Sanitarium called again. Ted had been found near Union Station in downtown Washington. The police had discovered him sitting on the steps of their precinct station in a thin jacket. Two aides were already on the way to pick him up.

Ted had, most assuredly, a proclivity for being found near police headquarters. Perhaps it meant he really did want to live, really did want to survive, really did want to get well after all, but that occasionally his despair drove him to episodes such as these. I would need to be patient, whatever he did. I had to remember that he was suffering far more than I—infinitely more. Perhaps, in his warped way, he even felt he was doing the best thing for me.

Such episodes, however, drove us apart. I went to see him the next day and found him unbearable. He was the martyr, the poor abused husband who had almost frozen to death

167

walking eleven miles in a snowstorm in his thin jacket. He had not been invited to my party, he said, so he stood out in the street, looking up at my window, feeling left out and unwanted, and decided that my life would be better off without him. But my god, did I realize how cold he had been? Did I know he almost had pneumonia? Did I know how alone and cold and sick he really was? Didn't I even care?

I could scarcely contain myself, and it was impossible to reason with him. No, I had not invited him because I felt the decision of whether or not to attend would be too upsetting for him. Would he really have come even if I had? Or would he have agonized over it for days and finally arrived when dinner was half over? Who had forced him to take an eleven-mile hike in the snow without overshoes or topcoat? Was I responsible for that?

He heard nothing. There he was, he continued, in his thin jacket, the snow seeping down his collar, his fingers numb. . . .

I knew honestly that the main reason I had not invited Ted was because I felt it would be too upsetting to me, not to him. This was a party for my friends, the ones who had helped me so often, and I wanted them to enjoy themselves, wanted to repay them somehow. What kind of a party would it be with a man who arrived late, declared that his food was poisoned, or paced from window to window while the others sang? But I felt no guilt this time. Miraculously, I did not feel responsible.

Letters between the Morenos and me were also becoming increasingly tense. They lamented the fact that Ted was here rather than there. They criticized the doctors, the treatment, the climate. . . . All Ted needed, they said, was God, and Mr. M. repeated his determination to stop all payments on May 1.

For my part, I could not have handled it worse. I decided that truth could win out over sentimentality, that the facts —as I saw them—would triumph over ego if I could just find the right words to convince them. In a last-ditch effort to reach Mr. M., or perhaps, unconsciously, to defend myself, I tried to explain slowly and patiently, without accusation, how Ted had got where he was. I reiterated all the things Ted had told me about his childhood and adolescence—the lack of playmates, the emphasis on books, the prohibition on girls and dating, the aloneness, the absence of a normal life. . . . I felt that if Mr. Moreno could just look objectively at the past, he would feel more responsible for Ted's treatment, more tolerant of the doctors and of me. I thought he would seek to make amends for the lousy life his son had had, and would write a contrite letter to Ted, announcing that he would support him in whatever would make him happy—that Ted's life was his to choose and plan and to live as he thought best.

How could I possibly have been so obtuse? To criticize their narrowness, their rigidity, their contradictions was to criticize everything they had ever been. Even to insinuate that if they had lived their lives differently Ted might not be where he was was to make them responsible for destroying the one thing they had managed to produce together, and what parent can accept that? Could I, had it been me?

Never for one moment did I believe that they had purposely set out on a course to cause pain and suffering to their only child. Everything they had done, no doubt, had been done with the best of intentions. They had encouraged him to be brilliant, to be chaste, to be rigid and single-minded because they desperately believed that this was best for him, or for them, or for, perhaps, the world. They had not reckoned with the possible emotional cost. It had taken them by surprise, and they could not cope.

And what if, after all, they were not to blame? What if it was all a chemical imbalance, a hereditary fluke that made them suspicious and secretive, that drifted down in the bloodstream from one generation to the next and would be cured some day not in the quiet counseling rooms of the Sanitarium or on the sterile white shock tables in the veteran's hospitals, but by a pill or an injection or a change in diet? I could not, knowing the Morenos and the life Ted had lived, believe that this was so, but neither could I prove it was not.

My letters did not work the magic I had hoped for, of course. They did not produce the outpouring of magnanimous remorse and concern I had imagined. My letters simply mortared up the wall between us, increased their resentment, deepened the gulf, and made them more determined than ever to put the blame elsewhere. Ted's breakdown came, after all, while he was living with me, not with them.

If I wrote that Ted seemed to be improving, they attributed it to Mrs. Moreno's prayers and her unique relationship with the Heavenly Father. If I wrote that Ted was unusually despondent and uncommunicative, it was because the Sanitarium was obviously the wrong place for him, the doctors godless, and what did I expect, being a Unitarian?

The weekly sessions with the social worker became my salvation. Slowly she pushed me toward decisions that would have to be made. Bit by bit, she made it clear that Ted might not be what I expected him to be when he left the Sanitarium, that what the hospital considered an adequate recovery might not be at all what I considered adequate for a husband.

For the first time I began to get a glimpse of what lay ahead. Despite the success of many patients, including Bill Goldberg who was now in medical school and doing well, there were others who graduated to the outer community but never got much beyond it—patients who lived strange, unpredictable lives, supported from afar by their wealthy families. True, they managed to exist outside the Sanitarium; they were no longer babbling incoherently, but they weren't exactly an employer's dream either. They dressed, some of them, in several layers of clothing, walked endlessly back and forth from one end of town to another, or slept all day and stayed up at night making phone calls around the country. But they were successful in that they no longer tried to swallow Drāno or immolate themselves. They succeeded in making a daily trip to the drugstore unaccompanied. And their relatives were happy to continue supporting them for life as long as they just didn't come home and embarrass them there. But this would never be enough for me. I wanted to *bear* children, not to inherit a fully grown child to take care of for the rest of my natural life.

That Ted would never go back to school for a Ph.D. I knew and accepted. That he would never teach college I realized too. That he might take a very common job in a common business somewhere was acceptable to me. But could he even do that? Could I count on him to make decisions, to stand on his own feet? Could I plan for children? Or would we live on a sub-level of society, afraid of ever leaving a simple routine, always in the shadow of that never-never land of Communists around the corner, waiting for something to set it off again?

Ted began to talk about coming to live with me and going on outpatient status. He had begun staying with me already over the weekends, and though he appeared nervous and distracted, he did not show any especially bizarre behavior. Knowing the desperateness of our financial situation, the hospital was willing to try, so in early spring, aides helped Ted move his clothes back to my apartment. He wanted to work, to make a contribution of some sort, he said. With the help of the social worker, he got a part-time job in the office

171

of a dry-cleaning plant and took the bus to work in the mornings. He spent four afternoons a week at the Sanitarium in therapy, arriving home an hour or so before I came in for the evening. But there was no particular joy in the new arrangement. We had been disappointed far too often to be elated at this.

It was a bold plan, a brave plan, a plan of optimism and hope and faith in the healing process of the human mind. But it didn't work. I began coming home to find Ted in the rocker, obviously agitated, maddeningly cracking his knuckles, sweating, trembling, his lips dry and his voice shaky.

"They're coming for me tonight," he whispered finally one evening. "They're angry because I'm living with you. They won't let me succeed. They won't stop, ever, until I'm dead. I know it now."

"Ted, Ted," I pleaded, like a broken record, "you're going back to your old ways of thinking. Can't you understand that the punishment you're talking about is coming from yourself?"

Is that any easier to take, I wonder? Isn't it always more comforting to know that the danger is out there somewhere, than to realize that it is coming from inside—that one's own mind, in fact, has turned traitor?

He grabbed my arm and pulled me down beside him, whispering so the radiator couldn't hear. "Phyllis, if you really love me, you'll help me find a chance to get away. They won't just kill me, they'll torture me first—long, slow torture." His voice trembled. "They plan to cut me up in little pieces, a section at a time."

I sat down beside him. "How long have you been feeling this way, Ted? When did the fears begin? A week ago? Or ever since you came to live with me?"

He gave a cynical smile. "The fears never stopped," he

answered. "I've never for a moment believed they weren't true."

My lungs felt cold, as though I had inhaled ice water. "Have you told your doctor about them?"

"Are you crazy? I'm not that dumb. Do you think they'd have let me out of there if I had? I play it smart. I tell them what they want to hear. I haven't talked about the Communists for months. That's why they let me out. But you've got to help me, Phyllis."

To put Ted back in the hospital was out of the question, since his father had withdrawn all financial support. Ted insisted he would not go even if I tried to readmit him. They had not helped him before, he declared, and could not help him now. We had already used up six thousand dollars of my uncles' money. It would have to be outpatient status or nothing, and obviously, it was not working. Ted had fooled even his doctor. I did not think I could stand any more.

For another week I debated with myself. One theme which had recurred again and again in our marriage was this: whenever things seemed to be going best for Ted, whenever he succeeded or was close to success, whenever things were going the best between us, he soon became upset and agitated. To enjoy sex, good food, friends, and to make a success of his work or school seemed to mean that retribution was in order —if not right then, eventually.

Perhaps what had been happening the last three years— the periods of tenderness and remorse alternating with surly belligerence—were only exaggerations of what he'd been feeling since the day we married, periods of passion and tenderness alternating with periods in which he criticized me unmercifully. The attentive, considerate, gentle lover he had been before our marriage became tyrannical once the marriage was actually consummated. The competent insurance underwriter who pleased his superiors had become petulant and unpredictable when offered a raise. The highly successful student who had graduated from the technological institute with honors became paranoid after he had been accepted back into the University for a doctoral program. And now that he had left the Sanitarium and returned to our bed, he was being haunted by warnings that he had better clear out.

Did the demons inside him refuse him any pleasure, success, or comfort? Did they take a dim view of anything that would make him happy? Was the only escape for his tormented imaginings to leave me and live the ascetic life of celibacy? Perhaps that was why he played the martyr and identified with Christ, with Mozart, with J. Alfred Prufrock, even:

> And I have known the eyes already, known them all—
> The eyes that fix you in a formulated phrase,
> And when I am formulated, sprawling on a pin,
> When I am pinned and wriggling on the wall,
> Then how should I begin
> To spit out all the butt-ends of my days and ways?
> And how should I presume?

He knew the poem by heart. In his own eyes, he was a great man, but nobody knew it. No one would let him succeed. And so he was doomed forever to walk through two-foot snowdrifts in a thin jacket.

He began missing the bus to his job and came back home instead. He broke appointments with his analyst at the Sanitarium. He refused to do anything except sit in the rocker, waiting for the inevitable. He did not sleep, but spent the nights prowling about, watching out of the windows.

I would lie in bed and see him standing there in the

moonlight, crying silently with his mouth open so as not to wake me, and I would bury my face in the pillow and weep too. He saw his career, his education, his pleasures, his wife, his very life slipping away before his eyes and he was powerless to stop them. The fears and the pain had paralyzed him into inaction. He was damned if he succeeded and damned if he didn't.

We had not yet tried a real separation. Perhaps, if Ted returned to some sort of pleasureless existence, the worries would lessen. It would certainly be easier on me, and I had to admit this frankly to myself. I could not go on night after night with little sleep as I had in the past. It was time to think about my own health. I suggested a separation to Ted, but he was powerless to decide. So I insisted that he go.

He went out one day and found a room above a pool hall. I helped him move his things. We said good-bye like robots, as though it were only temporary. Then I went home and slept an entire weekend.

What is it like to separate with the certainty that it is permanent, after eight years of marriage? What does it feel like to abandon someone—to walk out of his life when he is most dejected and alone?

What it felt like was a total absence of feeling. I was drained. I had no energy even to mourn. I was drained of regret, of hope, of sadness, of memories, and went to sleep ridiculously early each night without having to worry about what Ted was doing in the kitchen, what the sounds in the hallway might mean, and how long the water in the bathtub had been running. I did not have to wonder if I'd remembered to hide the steak knives in the linen drawer.

The following Friday, the social worker told me that Ted had asked to be discharged completely from therapy. In a statement about Ted's mental competency, his doctor wrote:

On admission he was acutely disturbed, but in time he improved to the point where it was felt quite feasibly that he could live outside the immediate hospital setting. Toward the end of his stay, he was employed and had improved to the extent that his fulminating symptomatology was no longer extant. In spite of strong recommendation that he continue in treatment, he declined. . . .

And an accompanying statement by the clinical administrator read:

At the time of discharge, he appeared to be mentally competent. There was no indication that he had a gross thinking disorder, there was no evidence of delusional ideas, and it appeared that he might be able to continue some sort of work. . . .

I did not tell the doctors that Ted's fulminating symptomatology had simply gone underground during his stay there. Perhaps because I knew it would not affect the outcome, perhaps because they had tried so hard and I did not want to disappoint them, and perhaps because I sometimes wondered if Ted put on his show of terror for me alone as a way of making me miserable, and that, in the calm, clinical atmosphere of the Sanitarium, he had *not* believed those fantasies. But how could the good doctor have been so mistaken? How could he have believed that merely because Ted did not talk about the Communists they had ceased to exist inside his head? I did not know, and it seemed futile to ask. They had done the best they could.

Ted and I had divided the bank account, what little was left, between us, so that we each had two hundred dollars. The debt to my uncles rested on me alone. I did not hear from Ted nor check on him. I knew that whatever news there was would be bad and I desperately needed a rest from emotional upheaval. But after several weeks, when my body had recuperated and I began staying awake in the evenings,

I sat alone in the rocker where Ted had sat, remembered his touch, his voice, and the look in his eyes as the terror mounted inside him, and was relieved to discover that I could still cry. The pain, I realized, was just as intense as when he was there.

The social worker was not surprised at my decision to separate. She felt it was time I began putting my own life together again, to decide what was going to happen to me. By mutual consent and with relief on both sides, I left my job at the education association and decided to spend my days writing and my evenings going to school. I would concentrate on children's stories, writing for the children I had never had.

"What about your sex life?" the social worker said. "I think it might be comforting, as well as helpful, for you to establish a relationship with someone. Perhaps Bill Goldberg. . . ."

Social workers have a way of forcing you rather quickly back into life. I needed sex, it was true, and had always found Bill attractive. But what do you say to a man who has formed a gentle, protective relationship with you, more like fond cousins than lovers? At what point does the warm smile take on a provocative meaning and the hand clasp linger? It seemed somehow incestuous.

The fact was, I needed more than sex. I needed a total relationship, concern, commitment. I met Bill on the street several days later and told him that Ted and I had separated, and then there was an awkward pause. I felt as though I were advertising myself, and was embarrassed. I felt he could read my eyes. But I had experienced the tingle of being single again—the sense of being attracted and attractive. I wanted to belong and be loved.

I became quickly involved in work and school. I wrote systematically, keeping a book of all my markets, listing word counts, special needs, and deadlines. I wrote stories and articles for every season, on every social problem known to man—on blindness, diabetes, alcoholism, and madness. I wrote fiction for five-year-olds, twenty-year-olds, and people in their eighties. I wrote comedy and tragedy, verse and prose, plays and open-ended discussions. I wrote anything anybody could possibly want, and continued night school, supported by magazines never found on the newsstands. I would get a degree in clinical psychology, I decided. I would devote my life to succeeding with other people where I had failed with Ted.

There is something about a woman alone—a woman who has been had—that assumes a woman desperately in need of sex. Above everything else, it is assumed, she needs a romp in bed to cure depression, insomnia, loneliness, grief, guilt, and all the various moods and conditions that accompany trauma. Men seem oblivious to the fact that a woman can masturbate quite easily to relieve her physical tensions and that she is not simply a coiled spring, stretched to the limit, waiting for a huge erection to come along and release her.

What she needs, even more than something in the vagina, is tenderness, compassion, concern. She needs to be rocked and held, caressed and comforted. She needs to know that she is a part of someone's future, that someone needs her in turn.

I had had enough of one-night stands with Ted—one moment of love followed by uncertainty and recriminations and the swell of loneliness beginning all over again. I had had enough aimlessness and lack of direction, of upheaval and change. I wanted to know where I was going, what I was going to become. I wanted to know that my life made sense, and I discovered that men came in all types, in all degrees of depth.

"What's the matter with you?" one man asked. "How

178

long's it been since you had any?" The appalling male ego. The more that men insisted we be intimate, the more interested I became in Bill Goldberg who did not rush me at all. But by this time he had found a woman of his own.

I had a date one evening with a handsome bachelor school teacher who was a model of gallantry through half an evening of conversation, good food, and laughter. But then, when he put one hand on my knee and announced that we would spend the rest of the evening in my apartment, I knew that I was to be the pièce de résistance and my defenses were up. By the time we reached home, I told him he had better not come up, that I felt the need of getting to bed early. I found myself pinned against the house, his bulging trousers pushing in my dress, his tongue going in and out of my mouth as he groaned out his desire. And all at once it seemed too funny for words. His gallantry had been such a sham. He expected me, obviously, to disrobe right there in the azalea bushes, so passionate I was to become. The harder he pushed, the less I wanted him. We were right outside the landlady's window and I knew she was listening to the whole bit.

When I still refused, he broke away from me, announced the evening a total loss, and left, and I could only agree. The dinner, the conversation, had been a bribe, nothing more. I felt as though I had deprived a small child of his dessert.

And then, through the maze of varsity men hulking across campus, the playboys and the nonstop-talking intellectuals, through the clutter of married students who felt that just because we had studied together they were entitled to a good lay before an exam, I met a quiet, mature man, a professional viola player who was also working on a degree in clinical psychology. He seemed everything that had first attracted me to Ted, but he was also at ease socially, was self-assured, and a man of many interests. He called and we made plans to go out, but before we had even got to know each other well, he was killed in a plane crash. I felt electrified with the shock of it, numb with the realization that tragedy could strike again so quickly. Would it always be like this—a number of men I cared nothing about, but grief for those that I did?

I would immerse myself in my work, I decided. I would read the hundreds of books I had never had time to read, learn to love Shostakovich, make pottery, write a novel, sing, take a course in Chinese cuisine, travel, get a job in clinical psychology, finish my own psychoanalysis, and keep perpetually busy. And then I fell in love.

Just when I had convinced myself that my career was all-important and I could adjust to the role of the single woman, I met a man who was intelligent, gentle, concerned, and didn't care at all about my birthmark.

Panic set in. I began looking over law books to learn about the possibilities for divorce in various states. What I discovered, in this era before the no-fault divorce laws, was that insanity was grounds for divorce only under the most rigid conditions. In almost every state, the psychotic spouse must have been insane for a prescribed number of years, usually five, the years must have been consecutive, the spouse must have been confined during that time to an institution, and three doctors must have declared the person incurable.

What would the judge say about a spouse who functioned reasonably well one week but went bananas another? What about a spouse who was in and out of hospitals at six-month intervals, or who was confined to an institution for four years and eleven months but was no better off when he left than when he entered? And where on earth would a lawyer find three psychiatrists—or two—or even one—who would pronounce a case incurable and hence rob that patient of hope? I was upset and anxious in the months that followed, and yet my marvelous friend was patient, and listened with amused tolerance to my elaborate plan to move to the Virgin Islands where one of the grounds for divorce was simply "insanity occurring after marriage."

But I was frightened of other things too. What had attracted me to Ted in the first place, a man who was destined several years later to be incapacitated by terror? It was obviously more than quiet intelligence and soft sweaters. What attracted me also to Bill Goldberg, a man who had been through the depths of suicidal cravings and had recovered? And what attracted me now to this new person that made him different from the men in the sports cars with their standard line about how much I needed them? Was there a certain sensitivity which I loved in these men that bespoke not only depth and intensity and soul but a proclivity for insanity as well? But this man did not go mad, and he stayed.

He was very tall—taller than Ted, even—slim, considerably older than myself, and he did not talk all the time. He was a great listener, an absorber, a reflector of feelings. He also had a Ph.D. Was I hung up on men with doctorates, I wondered? Did I feel that only a man like that could possibly understand me? Whatever, I knew I wanted marriage now as much as a year ago I had felt it to be impossible ever again. But I was sickened with the feeling that I'd found love— the original, unexpurgated edition—but would never be able to call it mine, that this was the way it would always be when I met a man I cared about—insanity, plane crashes, an endless wait for an impossible divorce.

The occasional mail which came for Ted, forwarded by me to his new address, suddenly began to come back. I drove to his rented room and asked to see him. He had left, they said. No forwarding address.

My feelings became a mixture of fear for Ted and what

might have happened to him, sadness for the person he used to be, panic over my own situation, anger at the complexity of marriage and divorce laws, and guilt over having entered so wholeheartedly into a wildly loving relationship while Ted—wherever he was, or whether he was at all—was miserable. I poured out my guilt to the social worker. I was still married, I told her, yet I'd met this man. . . .

"Phyllis, you certainly have a right to have friends," she insisted.

But he was more than a friend, more than a companion. He was a very big part of my life at that point, and there is nothing that increases longing for someone like having an obstacle in the way.

"Just be discreet," the social worker cautioned as I left her office.

I was leaving it, in fact, for the last time. As Ted was no longer a patient at the Sanitarium, I had long since ceased to be entitled to conferences with the social worker, and I knew I would miss them greatly. She suggested a particular psychiatrist to help me make the transition from being married to being single to possibly being married again, and her choice of doctors was excellent. Twice a week he helped me spread my anxieties out before us and examine them till they were no longer so frightening, to separate the real worries from imagined ones, the probable from the possible, and to weaken the feeling of responsibility for Ted's future that seemed to incapacitate me at times.

Life for me zigzagged between a billowing joy and a deepening despair that it wouldn't last. Divorce seemed legally impossible. Then I received a call from a woman in Washington, D.C. A man named Ted Moreno had taken a room there a month ago, she said, and she was very worried about him because he never went out or seemed to eat. She was afraid he might be ill. She had taken the liberty of searching through his things and had found my name and address in his wallet. Was I related in any way? Would I come?

I came.

Ted had lost a drastic amount of weight. He was lying on his back on the bed, fully clothed, and his white shirt had not been changed for days. He had a new growth of beard, and looked anemic.

"Hello," he said when he saw me, and smiled.

No matter how thoroughly one insists that a relationship is over, it is never quite ended. No matter how much one wants to begin life anew, the past is never quite forgotten. No matter how strongly I had promised to remain detached, my heart cried out when I saw him, wept for him and for all that he might have been, for what we could have had together. I wanted to take him in my arms like a frightened little boy, to rock him and croon to him, but I knew I could not, ever again.

I asked him how he was doing, whether he had any money, when he had eaten last. He said he was doing fine, that he still had money left, and he wasn't hungry. I asked if there was anything I could do for him. No, he replied, he would be all right. After eight years of marriage, there was nothing to say, and yet there were worlds to say.

I told Ted that if there was nothing more I could do for him, there was something he could do for me. I said that I wanted to start a new life for myself if I could, and that it was best we each be entirely free. He nodded, his eyes misting up, and I tried not to look at him. I said that divorce was possible in Maryland after a separation of two years if both parties agreed. Would he, I asked, sign the papers if a lawyer sent them to him? He shook his head. He would sign nothing; it might be a trick. It might give the Communists the authority to carry him off. No, I could do whatever I liked, but he would do nothing at all.

"Even for me?" I asked. There was no answer. I went back downstairs and gave the landlady his parents' address.

Gradually I began to discover what the preceding years had done to me, though it was little compared to what they had done to Ted. When my fiancé came to visit in my apartment, I found I could not bear to have him walk behind my chair. I found that even with this man, whom I trusted and loved, I could not easily turn my back on him without a distinct feeling of uneasiness.

I did not like to see him use a hammer or knife. I could not go into the bathroom in the middle of the night without glancing into the shower stall to check for a hanging body suspended by a belt. I could not bring myself to listen to the records which Ted and I had so carefully purchased together.

Once I attended a community meeting at which a psychiatrist talked about how many more patients could return home sooner if society would just accept them, if relatives would just be more tolerant, more understanding. . . .

Did you know what you were saying, Doctor? You, who know the right thing to do and say to a disturbed patient? You, with your years of training and experience, who can keep out of those emotional traps that patients set for you, and who can always, at the end of the hour, ring for an aide to take the patient back up to third and out of your life again? You, who, after a day of irrationality and paranoia and delusions and panic, can go home to a sane family with plans for the future, and close the patient out of your mind till two o'clock the following day? What about us, for whom there is no bell to ring, no aide to relieve us? For whom there are no plans, no future?

A month later I was awakened at two in the morning by the persistent ring of my phone. *Ted is dead*, I told myself as I fumbled toward the hallway. And then, *someone has been hurt in an accident.*

Ted's voice came over the line, an unusually friendly hello. I tried to wake up, to see the clock, to make sense of where I was and what was happening.

"Ted! Where are you?"

"I know it's pretty late," he said. "I suppose I woke you."

"Yes, but where are you?"

"Dallas. I'm between flights. I decided to visit my parents in Albuquerque."

"You left Washington, then? You'll be in Albuquerque?"

"No, I *was* in Albuquerque. I'm on my way back. It was a mistake to go there. I want us to start all over again, Phyl. I want to get a job and go back to see the doctor at the Sanitarium. Could you meet me at the airport at six?"

My head reeled. I felt as though I had been struck, as though all the years he had crept around behind my chair had built up into one big hammer blow at the back of the head. How well I knew my cues. How well I had rehearsed my lines. How often we had played this very scene, and how well I knew the outcome. *Oh, Ted, I'm so glad. I just know you'll get well now.* Isn't that what I was supposed to say? Isn't that what I had said dozens of times before? Didn't my part call for a splendid show of trust and confidence and an immediate drive to the airport? He sounded so eager, so sure, so confident that this time it would work. He seemed so apologetic, so loyal, so loving. . . .

But had anything changed, really? The decision to come back—how sudden it must have been, how impulsive—the phone call at two in the morning. No one had even let me in on the plan. Shades of the sheriff's call from La Crosse. Shades of selling our furniture and starting out for the Big City only to turn back. Shades of running away, of moving,

185

regretting the move. . . . Would she fall for it again, do you think?

But this time something really had changed. Something really was different. I was different.

"I'm sorry, Ted," I said, and could hardly believe that the voice was mine. "I can't live that way anymore. I can't take it physically and emotionally. I just can't."

There was stunned silence from the other end of the line. "But it won't be the same this time, Phyl," he insisted. "It really won't. I know what I want to do."

"Ted, I've heard that over and over again, but it never works out."

There was a pause. There was no sobbing, no sniffling, but somehow I knew, as a wife of eight years knows, that Ted was crying. My heart screamed inside of me.

"I love you, Ted," I said. "I'll always love you. But I can't live with you again."

"I'm sorry, Phyl," Ted said finally, and now he was crying openly. "Good-bye."

"Good-bye."

I never saw Ted, or heard from him, again. But I received several letters from his mother:

I thought you should know that Ted is in the hospital again. When we found him in Washington, he was thin and undernourished with no one to take care of him. We persuaded him to come to Albuquerque for a visit, but after several days he wanted to return to you. We bought his plane ticket, but when he called you from Dallas and you refused to take him back, he returned to us, a very sad and broken young man. . . .

And still later:

. . . when Ted returned to us, unhappy and confused, we knew he needed medical help at once. He insisted that his life had lost its meaning, however, and refused to see a doctor. Judge

186

Joseph Miller had Ted placed in the county hospital and ordered a trial. Ted is extremely intelligent, but sick, and he must have help. Judge Miller appointed Dad to be Ted's guardian, to protect Ted's rights and property, and placed Dad under bond. Ted has been deemed mentally ill, and has been sent to Santa Fe. God willing, he will remain there until he has been cured completely and is rehabilitated to once more resume his rightful place in our society. One thing is certain: Ted looked more healthy yesterday than he has in the last three years, and is pleased with our beautiful state. He finally has the chance he needs to get well, without being pulled from one place to another, never being able to complete his cure. He eats and sleeps well, and even smiles again, Praise the Lord. . . .

I was slowly, carefully, being prepared for the part of the villain. All the years when Ted had lived with me instead of them, the grudge had grown and now it was they who were in control. All the letters seemed to date the beginning of Ted's madness with my refusal to take him back after his call from Dallas. Every failure that had happened before was attributed to my pulling Ted from "place to place." I had become the outlaw, daring to speak of divorce. To have taken Ted from them and then ultimately rejected him was a double rejection of them in their eyes. They seemed to feel that I would stop at nothing. I was told that it was Mr. Moreno's responsibility to see that Ted's possessions were returned to him, and that he would get a lawyer to get them back if necessary, as though they really expected me to fight over Ted's books and typewriter like a dog over a bone, to withhold the few things that might give him pleasure. Was this what growing up in the Moreno household had been like—threats accompanying every request—a fierce, unnecessary show of power by people who felt powerless?

The warnings continued: "All letters sent to Ted at the hospital are opened for inspection. Also those sent by him," they wrote. Did they actually think I might try to lure him away? Couldn't they realize that the marriage was over, that I no longer wanted to live with their son?

On the premise that he might be persuaded to sign the separation papers, my lawyer had sent them to Ted at his parents' address as soon as I found out where Ted was staying. But it was too late. In December, explaining why the papers were returned unsigned, Mrs. Moreno wrote:

> You must know by now that Ted was not served with the divorce papers which you sent. At this time he cannot sign anything. Dad signs everything for him and will continue to do so until he is declared cured, the Lord willing. . . . Ted has told us about the last time you visited him in Washington and that you requested a divorce and how deeply this hurt him. The look on his face spoke volumes. . . . Dad, of course, is extremely upset by all this, and we would be truly ill now if it weren't for the special prayers of our *real* friends. I need not tell you how hard it was for Dad to sign the papers committing Ted to a hospital, or what the whole episode means to us, as it concerns our very beloved son.

In January:

> Ted is most certainly improving, due to love and prayers, plus hospital treatment. He looks marvelous, has gained some weight, and all of my friends think he is very handsome. Everyone here loves him. Ted is delighted with New Mexico, and talks of settling here when he is completely well. Perhaps he will live in Santa Fe. He hopes to teach again, and that is a good sign. We gave him some book shelves for a Christmas gift, and he promptly rearranged his books and possessions in his usual methodical manner. As to your wanting a divorce, I quote Ted: "I believe marriage is forever, sacred unto death, in sickness and health, but I won't hold Phyllis against her will. I'm reconciled to whatever may happen. . . ."

I was trapped. The Morenos held all the cards and played them one by one. Ted would not hold me against my will, but he would not set me free either. His parents did not want me, but now they gloried in the fact that I was tied to them by name. I became ill of myriad psychological stresses—stomach trouble, diarrhea, hives, urinary infections, headaches. . . .

"You must live for yourself—live your own life," the dermatologist told me. But how? An invisible umbilical cord stretched from Albuquerque, New Mexico, to Rushville, Maryland. It was made of U.S. Steel and reinforced by the divorce laws of every state in the union.

In February, my lawyer made a final attempt. He wrote Mr. Moreno that my present situation of being married to Ted in name only, with no hope of having a normal life with husband and children, was making me ill. I was in therapy, he told him, and it might be extensive. Since a husband is responsible for his wife's medical bills, Ted was responsible for mine. And since Mr. Moreno was Ted's legal guardian, he was therefore responsible himself for whatever debts I might incur from my various doctors. He was sending him the divorce papers in hopes that Mr. Moreno himself would sign them as Ted's custodian, in order to relieve himself of all further financial responsibility toward me, as the best thing to do for all concerned.

We waited. I knew what Mr. Moreno thought about money. I knew how he abhorred debt and distrusted doctors. But still the wait seemed endless. Perhaps he would simply never reply. Perhaps I would go my whole life in limbo.

Then I received the last letter I would ever get from New Mexico, this one from Mr. Moreno himself. He wanted written statements from three doctors verifying that my present marital situation was indeed making me ill. My psychiatrist, dermatologist, and gynecologist rapidly complied. A week later, the lawyer called. The papers were signed. I would go to Montgomery, Alabama, for the final decree, and would be officially divorced in sixty days.

I had made it. I had actually survived. If nothing else, I had perseverance. Perhaps my ancestors hadn't been so ordinary after all. Perhaps my forty-four sane and sensible relatives had given me more stability than I had realized.

What does one think about alone on a train in a ridiculous ritual of obtaining residency in another state by merely staying overnight? What does one muse about in the passage from one life to a new one, one love to another, one husband, once cherished, to a new one, equally loved? What of old dreams and plans when new ones are in the offing?

One thinks of everything and of nothing. I could not even respond when the conductor said lightly, "Guess you're going down there a Missus and coming back a Miss, eh?" And then I realized that half the people on the train were doing the same thing. A passenger car of broken marriages, a baggage car of shattered dreams. Did he think I had just discarded Ted like a winter coat?

I do not know what finally happened to Ted. I know, as one knows who has been through it, that the letters I had received from the Morenos telling me of Ted's marvelous improvement had been written on the upswings of Ted's moods, and that I never heard about the depths. I knew that they, as I had been, would be elated one week at his seeming progress and shattered the next. I knew that little by little their hope would be eaten away until they no longer smiled. I knew, and pitied them in a strange kind of way. If making me the scapegoat had brought Ted peace, and them also, I would willingly take the blame. I was free now and Ted was theirs forever, and I could afford to be generous, though I doubted it would help. Friends who later visited in Albuquerque reported that Ted was alternately in and out of the hospital, leaving to live temporarily with his parents, and then breaking down again, getting menial jobs and then giving them up.

I married, and now have two sons. At the beginning I suffered anxiety attacks and nightmares which were finally resolved in therapy. I still check the shower stall when I go into the bathroom at night, but it is more out of habit than fear. I have reached the place where I can listen to our records again and enjoy them, though Mozart's *Requiem* has never been out of its jacket. And I am relaxed when people walk behind my chair. As Ted taught me to think, my new husband taught me to feel, and I am grateful to both.

It had been fifteen years since I last walked up the drive to the Sanitarium, and I recently took an autumn stroll back through the grounds. The mansion still looks the same except for the tiers of screened porches at the back which have now been enclosed. Other buildings have been added for the treatment of children and adolescents as well. It has the same still, serene look about it that it had when Ted was there—a great silence except for the occasional murmur of voices as a small group comes out of the elevator at the back and makes its way down the path to the craft shop. A single dry leaf falls off the tall oak tree over my head and scratches the bark as it makes its whirling descent, lying motionless then on the ground with the others. The front door opens and a thin woman comes out and crouches down in one corner of the patio, staring at me vacantly, the same look she gave me when I came to visit Ted fifteen years ago.

The pain, for me, gets dimmer as the years pass, and I hope it does the same for Ted. Unable to decide between his mother's and father's dreams for him, finding it impossible to fulfill his own, he chose the least frightening way out and gave up everything.

Perhaps, with this sacrifice, the fears will let him rest. Perhaps the Communists will go back to making it rain on someone else and let him be. Perhaps the adventure and eroticism and challenge and fulfillment that he once read about in books and tried, bravely, to capture for himself, will go back again to the printed page. And in the quiet of his room, with shirts hung up buttons facing left, books arranged in alphabetical order, if he sometimes remembers Prufrock and weeps, I—two thousand miles away—weep with him:

I grow old . . . I grow old . . .
I shall wear the bottoms of my trousers rolled.

Shall I part my hair behind? Do I dare to eat a peach?
I shall wear white flannel trousers, and walk upon the beach.
I have heard the mermaids singing, each to each.

I do not think that they will sing to me.